"*I'd never met Laci Peterson, and all I'd ever seen of her was a grainy photograph on the Internet. But I wanted to help her. I wanted to believe that she and her child were alive and that I could keep them alive and bring them home safely. It was the oddest feeling: I thought Laci Peterson needed me; I thought she was counting on me to bring her and her baby home.*"
Amber Frey

WITNESS

For the Prosecution of Scott Peterson

"Provides [a] deeper look into her affair with Scott Peterson."
Associated Press

"Seduced she was. And so are we."
Wisconsin State Journal

WITNESS

For the Prosecution of Scott Peterson

Amber Frey

ReganBooks

AVON BOOKS
An Imprint of HarperCollinsPublishers

The names of certain individuals included in this book have been changed to protect their privacy.

Photography credits
All photographs are courtesy of the author, except:

Text:
Page vi, page 46, page 104, page 158: AP Wide World Photos; page 128: Al Golub/Pool/Getty Images; page 208: Ted Benson/Pool/Reuters/Corbis; page 234: David Paul Morris/Pool/Reuters/Corbis

Insert:
Page 14: Getty Images; page 15 (top): Chris Hardy/*San Francisco Chronicle*/Corbis; page 15 (bottom left): Lacy Atkins/*San Francisco Chronicle*/Corbis; page 15 (bottom right): Lou Dematteis/Reuters/Corbis; page 16 (top): Al Golub/Pool/ZUMA/Corbis; page 16 (bottom): Vicki Ellen Behringer

Cover:
Amber Frey by AP Wide World Photos; Scott Peterson by AP Wide World Photos; Laci Peterson by Getty Images

AVON BOOKS
An Imprint of HarperCollins*Publishers*
10 East 53rd Street
New York, New York 10022-5299

Copyright © 2005 by Amber Frey
ISBN-13: 978-0-06-083413-5
ISBN-10: 0-06-083413-7
www.avonbooks.com

First Avon Books paperback printing: February 2006
First ReganBooks hardcover printing: January 2005

Avon Trademark Reg. U.S. Pat. Off. and in Other Countries, Marca Registrada, Hecho en U.S.A.
HarperCollins® is a registered trademark of HarperCollins Publishers Inc.

Printed in the U.S.A.

10 9 8 7 6 5 4 3 2 1

For victims of violence. And for their families.

"No temptation has seized you except what is common to man. And God is faithful; He will not let you be tempted beyond what you can bear. But when you are tempted, He will also provide a way out so that you can stand up under it."

1 CORINTHIANS 10:13, NIV

CONTENTS

....

••••••••••••••••••••••

"Can I trust you with my heart?"

I first met Scott Peterson on November 20, 2002, at the Elephant Bar, in Fresno, California. It was a blind date—my best friend, Shawn Sibley, had set us up—and I got there before he did. I took a seat on a bench in the glass-walled foyer, within view of the walkway, and every time someone approached I looked up. I had butterflies in my stomach. I had a feeling my life was about to change. Scott Peterson sounded absolutely perfect.

Shawn had met him at a convention in Anaheim. She had been very impressed. Scott was intelligent, good-looking, and very funny, and he seemed eager to settle down. "Do you think there's a special person that you're meant to be with forever?" he had asked Shawn. From anyone else, the line may have seemed like a come on, but Scott was different. Shawn had told him that she was in a committed relationship, and he never once made a single flirtatious comment, never once tried to cross the line. At the end of the business day, she and Scott joined a few people for drinks and dinner. At one point he joked about putting the words "Horny Bastard" on his business card, thinking it might help him meet women, but mostly he behaved like a perfect gentleman. By the end of the evening, Shawn had a plan. "There's someone I want you to meet," she said.

"Who?" Scott asked.

"My best friend."

Shawn called me the next day to tell me about Scott and to ask if she could give him my number. I was full of questions. "What did you say about me?" I began.

"That you were beautiful and a good person," Shawn said.

"What was he like? Is he nice? Is he cute?"

"Very cute. And he couldn't be nicer."

"And he's serious?"

"*Very.* He said he was looking for someone special, and he asked if I knew anyone who was interested in a committed relationship."

"And?"

"And I thought of you, of course."

I didn't hear from Scott for several weeks, and when we finally connected he couldn't have been sweeter. He asked if I was free for dinner the following evening, and we made plans to rendezvous at the Elephant Bar.

"How will I recognize you?" I asked.

"Well, I'm not very tall," he said. "And I have long, greasy hair and a big, loose belly."

"That's good," I joked back. "I'm real tall and I weigh about a hundred and sixty pounds."

"Really?" he asked, laughing.

"No, not really," I said. "I'm thin and small-framed, five foot seven and a half, with blond hair."

"Good," he said. "Then it won't be a problem if I walk up to every attractive blond in the place and ask if she's Amber."

Shortly after six on the appointed evening, Shawn came over to stay with my baby daughter, Ayiana. "Just remember that I have to be at work tomorrow morning," Shawn said, only half-joking.

"Don't worry," I said. "I know."

I arrived at the Elephant Bar with time to spare. At exactly four minutes after seven, as I sat waiting for Scott, a man approached and made eye contact. I thought it might be Scott—he *sort of* fit the description—but I had a bad feeling about him. "Please God," I thought, "don't let it be him." I looked away, and—much to my relief—he moved through the foyer and disappeared into the restaurant. A moment later, another man approached; in my heart I knew and hoped that this was Scott. He was a shade over six feet tall, in good shape, and he was wearing a well-cut suit. He stepped through the glass door and lit up when he saw me.

5

"Amber?"

"Scott?" I replied, getting to my feet.

He leaned close and gave me a small peck on the cheek. "Am I late? I'm sorry I'm late."

"Not at all," I said.

The plan had been to meet at seven, in front of the Elephant Bar, and to go to dinner from there, so we left and made our way to the parking lot.

"I was a little nervous about meeting you," Scott said en route, but he didn't look nervous to me. He was smiling, and he seemed somehow relieved. "Can I ask you a favor?" he said.

"What?"

"I've been in this suit all day. Would you mind very much if we went to my hotel so I could check in and shower and change?"

I didn't mind. It seemed reasonable. I left my car in the parking lot and we got into his Ford truck and drove to the Radisson in downtown Fresno. When we got there, he began to unload his things. There was a big green lock-box in the cab of his truck, and his luggage was stashed inside. Scott looked at me sheepishly, as if embarrassed. "Look at all this stuff," he said. "I practically live out of my truck."

We went inside and took the elevator to a room on the top floor. Scott put his luggage down and reached into a brown duffel bag and pulled out a bottle of champagne. He smiled, and I found myself thinking he had a very nice smile. He popped the cork and proceeded to pour each of us a glass. Clearly this was a man who planned ahead.

Scott had a sip and turned on the radio and excused himself and went off to take a shower. I nursed my champagne, singing to myself to pass the time.

When Scott emerged from the bathroom a few minutes later, he was wearing black slacks and a clean white T-shirt. He went off to get a blue dress shirt and was still buttoning it up when he rejoined me. I was wearing a black skirt and a blue top. "We match," I said.

"So we do," he said.

Then he seemed to remember something. He reached into the duffel bag again and pulled out a box of strawberries, and he dropped one into each of our glasses. I watched the champagne bubble up around it and I had another sip and looked at him. He was smiling again. It was a warm, friendly smile.

When we finished our drinks, we left the hotel and went to a Japanese restaurant on Shaw Avenue. We were led to a table, but Scott immediately excused himself. He returned a few minutes later to say he had arranged for a private room. He led the way over and we took our shoes off and stepped past the sliding bamboo

7

door. The room had one table, low to the ground, and we sat next to each other on the floor.

In no time at all, we were in the midst of drinks and dinner, and our conversation flowed easily. Scott told me all about himself. He said he was a fertilizer salesman, that his travels took him all over the world—from Cairo to Paris—and that he lived, alone, in Sacramento, in a big, 1940s single-family home. "I'd love to have pets, but I travel so much it wouldn't be fair to them," he said.

I told him that I hadn't traveled much at all, but that I hoped to some day. "I know this sounds a little crazy," I said, "but when I was in junior college, I took two years of Swahili."

"I don't think that's crazy at all," he said. "I think that's very cool."

Scott told me he had acquired a taste for wine and that he belonged to several wine clubs. This impressed me. I like good wine myself and have always wanted to know more about it.

"I have a nice collection of good wine at home," he said. "Every month, the various clubs ship me a few choice bottles."

As the evening progressed, Scott said that he was looking forward to settling down, but that he hadn't yet found the right person. The way he looked at me when he said that made me feel he might be wondering whether *I* was that person.

Then I told him about my work as a massage

therapist. He seemed genuinely interested and asked lots of questions about my clientele, hours, and techniques. I told him that business was good and that I was on the verge of going out on my own. I was working at a place called Backworks, but I was in the process of making arrangements to take a larger space at American Body Works.

As for my personal life, I admitted that I'd had my share of unhappy relationships, but that there was one very bright spot in my life: my daughter, Ayiana. She was twenty months old that very day.

Talking to Scott was easy. He told me about his mother, Jackie, who was ill with chronic bronchitis. He said he had a condo in San Diego, which was fully furnished, with a Land Rover in the garage, and that he was thinking of selling the entire package.

"I never use the place," he explained. "I found a couple who are interested in buying it just the way it is, including every last stick of furniture and the Land Rover."

As I listened to him, I grew more and more impressed. I thought, *This guy is hard-working, ambitious, and he makes a good living. He really has potential.*

We also talked about the coming holidays. Scott said he was going to be fishing in Alaska over Thanksgiving with one of his brothers, his father, and an uncle, and that he'd be spending Christmas in Kennebunkport with his family, as he did every year. After Christmas, he would be going to Paris with friends to celebrate the New Year, and then he'd take a week or two to do some business in other European cities.

I said I'd be spending Christmas with some close friends, a married couple I'll call the Bensons. "They're like a second family to me," I said. I told him that my parents had divorced when I was five, and that there had been a lot of drama and a lot of back and forth when I was a kid, and that my mother was remarried and my father had been in a relationship for a while.

At one point, as we were finishing dinner, he put his hand on my back—a quiet, pleasant gesture—and said he was really enjoying the evening and would like to see me again. Everything felt very natural. I felt a nice connection to him.

"When are you going to see me again?" I asked. "Sounds like you're going to be gone for a long time."

"Not that long," he said. "I'll be back before the end of January." That was as specific as he got.

Suddenly the hostess came in to tell us that they were getting ready to close for the night, and we were the last two people in the restaurant. She could see we weren't done talking, so she suggested we go next door, to the karaoke lounge. We went over and Scott ordered a pair of gin and tonics—not that we needed them—and he told me we should get up and sing.

"No way," I said. "I'm not getting up in front of people. I'm too shy."

"Come on!" he said. "I heard you singing in the hotel room, when I got out of the shower. You have a beautiful voice."

He really wanted to get up there and sing, and he kept pestering me, but nicely, and I looked around and noticed that there were only a few people left in the place. So I said yes. We decided to try our luck with "Islands in the Stream," which has two parts, male and female, and we launched in. We were terrible. I was laughing so hard I could barely catch my breath. But Scott kept singing, so I played along.

When the song was over, I apologized to the patrons for our performance—a couple of them actually clapped at this point—and we began to make our unsteady way back to the table. But a Frank Sinatra song came on, and I felt like dancing.

"I'm not a very good dancer," Scott said.

"Don't worry," I said. "I'll lead."

I was pretty tipsy by this point, so we didn't really dance much. We just sort of stood there

11

and swayed. It was nice, though. It felt good just being close to him.

When we went back to our seats, Scott looked at me and asked if I was a smoker.

"No," I said.

He leaned over and kissed me. "Oh yeah," he said. "You are definitely not a smoker."

A few minutes later, the lights went up and we realized it was time to go.

We got into his truck and drove over to the Food Maxx for a bottle of gin, which we also didn't need, then returned to the Radisson. I was in no condition to drive home, so I went up to his room. When we stepped inside, he turned and kissed me again, somewhat more passionately this time.

"I don't know if I'm ready to be with you," I said, but my resistance soon faded and I ended up spending the night. I liked him. I could see myself falling for a man like Scott Peterson.

In the morning, early, Shawn called me on my cell phone. She didn't ask any questions, but she reminded me that she had to go to work. We got dressed and Scott drove me back to my car, which was still in the Elephant Bar parking lot. There was a ticket on the windshield, and I gave it to him. "Here's a little memento for you," I said. I wasn't feeling all that good about myself, and about having spent the night, and I guess I was trying to be funny. But Scott didn't seem to think it was funny. He looked very serious. "I really want to see you again," he said. "Do you want to see me?"

"Yes," I said. "I do. I guess I just feel a little weird about last night. It felt like a one-night stand, and I don't do one-night stands."

"It wasn't a one-night stand," he said. "I know we just met, but I think we really connected. I really like being with you, and I want to spend more time with you and get to know you better. I'm sorry I have to leave town so soon."

"Will you call me?"

"Sure," he said. "I'm not real good about phones, but I'll try."

We kissed good-bye and I got in my car and drove off. I didn't look back. I felt certain we would see each other again.

I got home and told Shawn that I'd had a very nice evening, but she didn't have time for details. Then I took my daughter, Ayiana, to preschool, and made my way to Backworks.

Scott called later that day. He had gone to a meeting and was passing through Fresno again, and he wanted to come over and see me. But I was tired and I had more clients that afternoon. He said he understood and promised to call again.

The next day, Scott called and left a message.

"I'm kicking myself," he said. "I wish I could have seen you at least once more before my trip." He called a couple of days later to tell me that he was on his way to Alaska. He said he had picked up a book about nature hikes in California, and that there were some pretty amazing trails around Fresno. "Maybe we'll go on a hike when I get back," he said.

"That would be nice," I said.

On Monday, December 2, Scott called in the early afternoon and told me he was back in Fresno, not far from my house. "Are you ready for that hike?" he asked.

I gave him directions to my house and he got lost and called back and I guided him through the neighborhood. He arrived with some amaryllis and two bags of groceries. "I brought a little something for dinner," he said. "I hope that wasn't too presumptuous. I brought stuff for the hike, too."

"Not presumptuous at all," I said. "It sounds great."

"Where's the little one?" he asked.

"At school," I said. "I'm on my way to pick her up. You want to come with me?"

"I'd love to," he said, and he sounded genuinely excited.

We put the groceries away and he had nice things to say about my place. I was living in

Rolling Hills at the time, in Madera County, in an 800-square-foot guest house. It had one bedroom, and a tiled kitchen, and a big, open living room. Ayiana and I were very happy there.

We went outside and transferred the car-seat into his truck and went off to get Ayiana.

"How was Alaska?" I said.

"Beautiful," he said. "Look." He showed me a photograph of himself near a stream, holding a fish. It was taken at such a long distance that it was hard to make out much detail. "I'll have to take you there some day," he said.

When we got to the school, we went inside together and I briefly introduced him to the director, a close friend. Ayiana was very happy to see me, as always, and when we got outside she couldn't believe we were about to climb into a real truck.

"It's Scott's truck," I told her.

"Scott truck, Scott truck, Scott truck!" she squealed.

"She is so incredibly cute," Scott said, glowing. "Listen to her talk!"

My God, I thought. *This guy is perfect*. Scott picked her up to put her in her car-seat and Ayiana took to him right away. He told her we were going on a hike, and she repeated the word: "Hike, hike, hike!"

We drove to nearby Auberry—I'd been there many times before, but never with Ayiana—and we walked along a trail to a place called Squaw's Leap. Ayiana held both our hands all the way to the clearing, where we stopped to picnic on the snacks that Scott had brought along. He also had a blanket with him, and he laid it out on the grass. He seemed very happy. He couldn't stop grinning at me and Ayiana. "Look at me," he said. "I've got a rigor mortis smile."

It was very beautiful, but a little chilly, so we soon headed back. Ayiana was tired and Scott ended up carrying her most of the way. When we reached the truck, it was beginning to get dark, and we sat in the open cab to watch the stars come up.

"Let's see who can spot the very first star," Scott suggested, turning it into a competition. He won. A few stars later, Ayiana was fast asleep.

Scott talked about Thanksgiving and about families—and how complicated they were. "Some relatives you don't really like but you have to get along with them because they're family," he said.

"I know what you mean," I said. "Anyone who has a family knows."

Scott managed a half smile. I got the impression that one of his relatives was rubbing him the wrong way, but I didn't want to pry. When the temperature began to drop, we got back inside the truck and went back to my place.

The minute we walked in, Scott took me aside and told me that he had brought a little something for Ayiana. "I didn't know whether it was appropriate for me to give her a gift, so I thought I'd clear it with you," he said. I couldn't believe this guy: he was so considerate. I told him it was fine and thanked him for discussing it with me. "If you had given her a present when you first met, I would have questioned your motives," I said. "But since she already knows you and likes you, I'm sure it will be fine."

He gave Ayiana her present and she eagerly tore the wrapping to shreds. There was a beautiful book inside—a richly detailed Christmas pop-up book—and Scott sat her on his lap and went through it with her. They looked really cute together. I was so happy to see this side of Scott. When Ayiana began grabbing at the pop-ups, I worried she might rip them. "I think we'd better keep that beautiful book away from her busy little hands," I said. "At least until she's old enough to appreciate it."

The next thing I knew, Scott had started preparing dinner. He made an elaborate seafood lasagna. As soon as the pan went into the oven, he opened a bottle of wine—he'd brought that, too—and I took the cork from his hands. "I'm going to keep this," I said. "It feels like it means something."

I told him that a friend of mine had a huge

glass container at home filled with corks, and that he dated them and jotted down the names of the people he'd shared the bottle with. I thought it was a great idea: you could reach into your collection of corks and read the names and dates and think back to those particular evenings. I grabbed a pen. "I'm going to date this and put our names on it," I said.

"Did you save the cork from our first bottle of champagne?" he asked.

"No," I said. "I didn't think about it then."

"That's okay," he said. "There are plenty of corks to come."

I felt unusually comfortable around Scott, as if I'd known him for a very long time. I didn't feel I had to try to be anyone other than who I was, and it seemed as if he felt very much the same way. In a word, being with Scott was effortless.

He spent the night.

The next day, Tuesday, December 3, he called to say he was coming back into Fresno, and that he would probably be in town till morning. I had a client at 5:30 that evening, and Ayiana had to be picked up by 6:00 p.m. I had asked my mother to get her, but suddenly it occurred to me that Scott could pick her up. I realize I didn't know him very well, and that it seemed a little hasty, but I had seen them together and I had been very pleasantly surprised at the way Ayiana took to him. I had never asked anyone other than my mother to pick Ayiana up at school. I'm an intensely protective parent. But for some strange reason I didn't have the slightest hesitation with Scott.

"Would you mind getting her for me?" I asked.

"No, I'd be honored," he said. "I'm just worried she won't want to leave with me."

"She'll leave with you," I assured him. "She likes you. I think she'll be excited to see you."

I dropped the car-seat and the key to my apartment at Ayiana's school and went off to take care of my client. When I got home, at around 6:45, I found Ayiana in her high chair, happily eating dinner, and Scott nearby, busily chopping tomatoes for bruschetta. He had a glass of wine in his hand and he poured one for me and welcomed me home like it was the most natural thing in the world.

"How'd it go at school?" I asked.

"Great," he said. "I ran into your director friend and she was very nice, but they still checked me out at the front office, and even asked for my ID. I thought that was very cool. I like the fact that they're so security conscious."

I looked over at Ayiana—she was happy and smiling—then I looked back at Scott. This handsome man was beaming at me, and the place was filled with all sorts of wonderful, homey cooking smells. I felt like I had a family; a real family.

After dinner, we went out to get a Christmas tree. My dad had said I could borrow his truck, but with Scott's Ford outside I didn't need it. We bundled Ayiana up and drove to the lot and Scott picked a tree we all liked. I went to pay for it, and Ayiana and Scott stood by the small bonfire, staring at the petting zoo, which was all lit up. The man who owned the place made change and I joined them by the petting zoo, and before long the owner had wandered over and was smiling at us. I guess he thought we were a nice, happy family. "Your parents sure bundled you up nicely," he told Ayiana. Scott and I looked at each other, but neither of us bothered to correct him.

We took the tree home and set it up and I went to get the ornaments out of the closet. I returned to find Scott draped over the loveseat. It had been a long day—miles of road, hours of meetings—and he was tired. He looked so handsome and so comfortable, and he looked so much like he *belonged*, and I couldn't help myself: "Have you ever been married?" I asked.

"No," he said.

"Ever get close?"

"No," he said. "Never."

I didn't say anything, but my heart jumped a little. I was full of hope. I turned and began to decorate the tree and Scott asked me to tell him stories about the ornaments. Even *that* impressed me: the fact that he knew that Christmas ornaments are often connected to stories. I told him that I had been a preschool teacher for seven years and that most of my ornaments had been gifts from my students. My favorite was a little angel made out of a single clothespin. It had crinkly hair, a little cotton dress, and a tiny halo made of tinsel and wire. Ayiana kept pulling at the ornaments, so I began to replace them with her collection of Beanie Babies, but she tried to pull these down, too. Scott and I were laughing and having a good time.

"Baby, baby!" she said, yelping with delight.

The way Scott looked at her, and at me, and, well—it's hard to describe. He seemed so happy and peaceful. I went over and cuddled with him on the loveseat. He put his arm around me and pulled me closer to his warm body, and I felt as if I were about to melt. It had been a very long time since I'd felt that comfortable with a man. In fact, as I thought back on it, I realized that I hadn't been close to anyone for a long time. I really needed someone in my life, but I guess I'd been fighting it.

Still, I was lonely—and I couldn't deny it. My friends always said, "Oh, Amber—your life is perfect. You have Ayiana. You have a nice home. You have a great job. You have your independence. What more could you want?"

I guess they were simply trying to be supportive. Or maybe their relationships weren't all that great and they envied my strength and independence. But I was tired of being strong and independent. I wanted someone to lean on, someone to come home to.

I often took long walks, pushing Ayiana along in the stroller, and I'd see couples here and there, walking hand in hand, and I would think, "That's what I want. I want a partner." And I would have long conversations with God. I would say, "I know I have a lot to be thankful for—this beautiful daughter you've given me, this good life—and I know I shouldn't complain, but I can't help it: I'm lonely." And I swear that one night I heard God answering—not so much in a human voice; it was more of a feeling, really—and He said, "It's all right to feel lonely. You *do* need someone, Amber. And you'll find someone."

It was only a short time later that Shawn told me about Scott. "You know, I have never met anyone that I thought was good enough for you," she had told me. "But this guy is funny and smart and polite and good-looking and a real gentleman. And he's looking to settle down."

Shawn had always been very protective of me. She had been around when my last serious relationship fell apart, and she had seen me literally curled up in pain. And she had been there when I pulled myself out of my depression, and got back on my feet, and turned my life around. But she knew I was lonely.

"This guy is a great catch," she had told me. "If I wasn't in love with Tommy, I would definitely be seriously interested in Scott Peterson."

She was right. Scott Peterson was a great catch. And at that moment he was right there in my living room, in my loveseat, pressed up next to me. It felt good and right and very promising.

"What are you thinking?" I asked him.

"Nothing," he said, smiling. "That I'm so comfortable. Your home is very relaxing. I'm enjoying watching you and Ayiana. I'm happy." He yawned and looked at his watch. "I better get going," he noted. "I'll get a hotel for the night."

"Don't be silly," I said. "Stay here."

Shortly thereafter, Ayiana curled up in her favorite spot in the living room and was soon peacefully asleep. Scott and I retired to the bedroom, and—perhaps because I was feeling hopeful about Scott, perhaps because I so much wanted things to work out between us—I found myself talking to him about trust. "It's so much better to tell someone the truth, even if it's hard, than to tell a lie," I said. "Because even a tiny lie leads to mistrust. And once trust has been broken, it's hard to rebuild."

"I agree with you," Scott said.

"I find it a lot easier to deal with the truth, no matter how painful, than with lies."

I told him about an ex-boyfriend who had assured me that he wasn't into pornography, and how I'd come to discover a huge stash of dirty magazines in his possession. I didn't approve of the magazines, but that wasn't the real issue. The real issue was that he had lied to me about something so minor. If he could lie about that, he was capable of lying about anything at all. "That's why, for me, I'd always rather know the truth, whatever it is," I told Scott.

"That's an unusual quality," Scott said. "You're an amazing woman."

After we made love, and long after he had fallen asleep, I found myself clinging to him. I didn't know what I'd done to deserve this wonderful man. He was smart, charming, sexy. He treated me with respect and kindness. And he was absolutely great with Ayiana. I knew it was still early in the relationship, but I began to see us making a life together. Maybe I was rushing things—in my mind, anyway—but I was almost certain I was rushing to a beautiful place.

The next morning, while Scott was still asleep, I bathed and fed Ayiana and took her to school. I returned to find him in the kitchen, his hair still damp from the shower. "I think I really like you," I said, kissing him.

"I *know* I really like you," he replied.

I had an art show to attend the following night, at the Fresno Art Museum, and I asked Scott if he would come with me. By this time he had almost finished dressing and was getting ready to leave. I realized I missed him already.

"I wish I could," he said. "I have to go to San Francisco." He was going on business, and once that was taken care of he had arranged to go boating with some friends. He said he didn't expect to be back in the Fresno area before the weekend.

I was eager to see him again, so I told him that Shawn was having a party on December 11, for her fiancé, Tommy, and that I had a formal to go to on December 14, a fund-raiser, and was hoping that he would be able to go to that, too. He said he'd love to go to both.

He accompanied me to my new office, at American Body Works, on Sixth Street, and helped me set up. We put up my certificates and some racks, and I could see that Scott was handy with tools. I know it's silly, but this impressed me, too. We then set up my massage table, and I ended up giving Scott a massage. It was all very professional—I treated him as I treat all my clients—and when we were done we went to the bank drive-thru and Scott withdrew a large amount of money. He wanted to pay me for the massage, and I tried to refuse, but Scott insisted and even added a 20 percent tip. Then we went off to Whole Foods for lunch. I had the tortilla soup, which was great, and Scott told me that he loved to cook, and that he had this great big kitchen at home. "I'd really enjoy cooking for you," he said.

"I'd like that, too," I replied.

As we left Whole Foods, I saw a big stack of Pink Lady apples, and I told him that when I was pregnant with Ayiana I had been wearing braces, and I couldn't eat apples. I said that months later, when I finally bit into a caramel apple, it had been a big disappointment because it wasn't a Pink Lady. After lunch, we went our separate ways, and all I could think about was how much I enjoyed Scott's company.

On the 5th, I went to the art opening and ran into my friend Saki Vincent. She was a client, and a graphic designer, and a single mom, like me, and we had become pretty good friends. I told her all about Scott and admitted that I was pretty smitten, which I guess was obvious: I couldn't seem to keep the excitement out of my voice.

"You deserve someone good in your life," she said. "I hope he's the one."

The next day, December 6, Shawn was discussing business with a colleague and happened to mention Scott by name. The colleague knew the name: he had once interviewed with Scott for a job. He told Shawn that Scott was married and lived in Modesto. Shawn was sure he was mistaken, that it must be a different Scott Peterson, but he insisted: "I'm telling you, it's the same Scott Peterson. I met the guy."

As soon as she got off the phone, Shawn dialed Scott's number and got through and confronted him. "Tell me I didn't set my best friend up on a date with a married man?!" she said, already angry.

"What?!"

"I just got off the phone with someone who says he knows you. He says you're married and live in Modesto."

"That's crazy! It must be another Scott Peterson."

"I don't believe you," Shawn said. "I'm going to look into this. Amber is my best friend, and I don't want to see her get hurt."

Shawn got off the phone and logged onto the Internet and gained access to Sacramento County records. Within minutes, she discovered that Scott Peterson was indeed married and that he did indeed live in Modesto. She called him back, very angry now, and told him what she'd learned. Scott didn't answer right away, and a moment later she heard him crying.

"Scott? Are you still there? What's going on?"

"I'm sorry," he said, still crying. "I'm sorry I lied to you. It's just—I lost my wife. It's been very hard for me. I haven't fully dealt with it yet."

Shawn was horrified. She didn't know what to say. She stammered an apology of her own. "Oh my God. I'm so sorry, Scott. I had no idea."

"Please," Scott said. "I beg you: don't tell Amber. I really care for Amber, and I don't want to screw this up. Let me tell her myself. I want to tell her in person."

"Absolutely," Shawn replied. "That's fine. I just—you know—I just didn't want Amber to get hurt. That was the reason I confronted you. Amber isn't looking for someone to have sex with. She's looking for someone with whom she can spend her life."

"That is totally what *I'm* looking for," he said. "I mean it. I'm not going to blow this, Shawn. Please trust me. Let me tell Amber myself."

Shawn decided to respect Scott's wishes. He sounded genuine, and genuinely torn. And for good reason: the poor guy had lost his wife. Shawn had wanted to ask him how he had lost his wife—to illness? in an accident? to another man?—but it didn't seem appropriate. And she imagined she'd find out eventually, probably from me.

I didn't know this at the time, of course. Just as I didn't know that two days later, on December 8, Scott was looking through the classifieds for a fishing boat, nor that on the same day he was scouring the Internet for information on currents in the San Francisco Bay and began negotiating for the boat. The following day, Scott purchased the fishing boat for fourteen hundred dollars, then visited a sport fishing site to determine what kind of fish were in season.

That same day, Scott came to see me at home. This is how I recalled the visit for the police, several weeks later, when they came to my apartment. I was pretty nervous, which I know they understood, and it showed:

> "So he's wearing a blue suit and he had his International Rotary pin on and I said hi and . . . how are you, and he's like not good and I said what and he was just like, I really need to talk to you and I [said] okay. . . .
>
> " . . . he was very upset, very distraught about something he had done that was very devastating possibly to what could be a beautiful relationship and that he uh was just like I need you to come in here, he moved the chairs. He sat in that chair there, I was sitting there, he was sitting there and was pretty mad, was up pacing a little bit and [said], okay, well, what, I couldn't understand, well, what is it? And he said you know I really would just be so, it'd be so much easier if you just hated me and you didn't wanna see me again and, and I'd understand and, and . . . I just, I

29

hate myself so much right now. . . . Then he talked to me about lying and then, and then he goes I just . . . had such a horrible weekend this week and it wasn't fun for anybody 'cause I had this on my mind and I was like, What?! You know, and I'm holding his hand and he was crying, his stomach kept churning and he was having trouble swallowing and tears were pouring down out of his eyes. And he said, I lied to you about being, you asked me if I'd been married and I have, but it's . . . in my past and it's so hard for me, because I just, I've had such a hard time dealing with . . . and uh I said okay. And . . . I'm thinking well she's passed away you know, and . . . he goes you know I haven't said very much, but obviously you know that, you know, she's not with me and he goes . . . I wanted to talk, be able to talk to you about this and I was going to talk to you about this when I came back from Europe, but he was, this was on my mind and I had to let it all out, and I was like okay. And I go I'm sorry this was so hard for you to tell me and I thank you for sharing this with me. And, and I . . . there will be a time for you, you know, to share more and he's like . . . taking breaths and he's having trouble swallowing. He's like . . .

you're not mad and I said how can I be mad if something, you know, is . . . how can I possibly for . . . that's understandable if you have a loss. . . . And he goes, and, and he said uh this will be the first holidays without her. . . . "

It was terrible. There was one point, early on, just as he began to talk, when I said, "Geez, Scott—for a moment there I thought you were going to tell me you were married."

And he said, "No, no, no!" And he kept asking me if I was mad. And I told him no, I wasn't. How could I be mad? And he said, "You have no idea how hard this is for me. I never talk about her, with anyone. When I meet new people, I act like my marriage never even happened."

I was curious, of course. Who wouldn't be? But I was also concerned. When he said that this would be his first holiday without her, I realized that the loss was very recent, and I wondered whether he should take more time to grieve. I was thinking about him, not about myself, and I asked him, "Are you ready for a relationship with me?"

"God, yes!" he said.

I didn't see Scott again for several days, and I was feeling confused and a little fearful. He had lied to me, and it was hurtful, but I could understand why he had lied, and I had no right to stand in judgment of him, so I worked at putting it behind me. After all, he was the one who had suffered an unimaginable loss. It was my job to be there for him, and to be as understanding as humanly possible.

That following evening, December 10, Ayiana was running across the living room when she tripped on the rug and fell against the stereo cabinet, cutting her head open. There was blood gushing from her forehead and I grabbed a towel and called the landlord to ask him to take us to the hospital. It was only five minutes away, but my car was a stick shift, and I knew I couldn't manage it. He was home, luckily, and we rushed over to Valley Children's Hospital, where the doctors stitched her right up. I called Scott from the hospital and reached his voice-mail, but I didn't leave a message. I didn't want to upset him unnecessarily. Then I took Ayiana home and comforted her and put her to bed.

Scott came over the following afternoon and behaved like a perfect angel. He was incredibly sweet to Ayiana and even changed her bandage and later asked me how I had handled the accident: "I mean, you know, as a mother—to see your daughter bleeding like that? How do you handle something like that? It must be incredibly hard to see your daughter in pain." And I said,

"You don't even think about it. You just do what needs to be done. I guess it's maternal instinct."

That was the night of the party for Shawn's fiancé, but we also had the formal to think about, so while Ayiana was at school we went down to the Fashion Fair Mall to rent a tuxedo for Scott. We went home and I went to get Ayiana and we hung out, and when it was time for the party I slipped into a pair of blue jeans. Scott went in casual pants and a blue shirt.

I distinctly remember what he wore because I saw him in this same shirt several weeks later, on the news, when the networks were busy reporting on his missing wife, Laci. One of the photographs showed Scott and Laci together, and Scott was wearing that very same shirt.

Just before we left for the party, I called Shawn and asked her if she could try to snap a photograph of Scott, Ayiana, and me. I asked her to be discreet, however, because the photograph was going to be the centerpiece of a Christmas ornament I intended to make for Scott.

"You got it," she said.

"Thanks," I said. "I really appreciate this."

The party was at Shawn's house, about half-an-hour away, and there were plenty of other children there. It was lots of fun and everyone was taking pictures, but the battery on Shawn's camera died and I never got the shot I wanted. Instead, there was a photograph of Scott sitting in a chair, holding a beer, with me leaning toward him. When Scott later went on trial for murder, that photograph was entered as evidence.

That night, however, I was with a different Scott altogether. The Scott at my side was outgoing and personable and charming and very much able to take care of himself, and clearly everyone really liked him. I didn't get much of a chance to talk to Shawn—she was too busy being a good hostess—but at one point I got the feeling she had something to tell me. It was the way she was looking at me. "What?" I asked her at one point. But before she could answer Tommy came by and dragged her away.

When the party was over, Scott came back to my place and again spent the night.

The next day, December 13, Shawn came in for a massage, and while I was working on her I sensed a small level of discomfort. I had a hunch she was keeping something from me, and I asked if she had forgotten to tell me something about Scott. She was very upset, and the truth came pouring out of her. "I found out completely by accident," she said. "And I really wanted to tell you. But Scott was crying. And he begged me to let him tell you about his wife himself. So I'm sorry. I feel like I've lied to my best friend."

I told her I totally understood and that I wasn't really mad at her. Shawn is a good per-

son, and this was an unusual situation. I understood why Scott had been reluctant to discuss
his loss with either of us. He was still grieving.
Shawn understood this, too, but she wasn't
happy about it. "He lied to both of us," she said.

"I know," I said. "But there were extenuating
circumstances."

"I'm aware of that," she said. "But it still both-
ers me. You should be careful."

I asked her if he had told her how his wife had
died and she shook her head. "Did he tell you?"
she asked.

"No," I said.

On December 14, the night of the fund-raiser, I
took Ayiana to my mother's house and went
back to my place to wait for Scott. I was trying
not to think about the conversation with Shawn,
but it still gnawed at me. She had found out
about Scott's past by accident, and Scott had only
come to me with the truth after she'd confronted
him. This didn't exactly inspire confidence.

Scott arrived with a dozen red roses. "I hope
you have plenty of vases," he said, and he suddenly pulled another two dozen roses from his
duffel bag, where he'd covered them with a coat.
He had also brought two bottles of champagne.

As I began to put the roses in a vase, he took a
single stem and set it on the table.

"Why'd you do that?" I asked.

"I'm glad you asked," he replied. "While I was

in San Francisco, this one rose was all I could think about the entire time."

He snipped off the stem and began rubbing the petals against my skin, and he began to kiss me. It was very hot, and the petals were now circling my breasts, but it was time for us to get ready. Plus I had some things on my mind, and—much as I tried to keep my thoughts in check—I couldn't help myself. "Listen, Scott," I said, "I have something to ask you."

"What's that, sweetie?"

"I talked to Shawn. She told me how she found out about you being married. I was just wondering: Would you have told me the truth if Shawn had never found out?"

"Oh, sweetheart," he protested. "Of course I would have. You *know* I would have. I was going to tell you everything when I got back from Europe. It's—it's just been very hard for me is all."

I wasn't looking at him when I posed the question. I didn't want to put him on the spot, and I didn't want to be confrontational, so I had made every effort to sound casual. I hadn't wanted to catch him off guard, and I wasn't watching for it. On the other hand, weeks later, when I thought back on it, I realized that he must have been ready for it. After all, Shawn was my best girlfriend, and he probably assumed that she couldn't possibly have kept the secret to herself.

"I am so, so sorry," he said. I was looking at

him now, and his eyes glistened with tears. "I never meant to hurt you."

He kept going on and on, and I felt very badly for him, so I did the only thing I could do: I forgave him. The fact is, it was easy to understand why he hadn't told me. And it made perfect sense. I'd never gone through such a monumental loss. I had no idea how it must have felt, nor how I would have dealt with a similar situation in my own life. I didn't want to stand in judgment. And I wanted to believe him. So I simply accepted his explanation.

Then I told him I had only brought it up because I wanted to be sure about him. "Can I trust you with my heart?" I asked him.

"You know the answer to that already."

"No, I don't," I said. "That's why I'm asking."

"You know," he said. "I live a certain lifestyle, and I can see you living that lifestyle, too. When I get back from Europe, I need to make some decisions. Can you say yes to me without question?"

I didn't understand why he refused to answer me directly, so I repeated my question: "Scott, can I trust you with my heart?"

And he answered exactly as he'd answered before: "You know the answer to that already."

It was very tough for me. I liked Scott, and I wanted a relationship, but I was still worried about his state of mind. He had such a charming way about him, yet he seemed oddly reluctant to answer some of the simplest questions. Then again, I knew he was in pain, and that the loss was recent. I wanted to be forgiving, for both our sakes. It had been a long time since I'd been genuinely interested in a man, and I was genuinely interested in Scott. I didn't want to get carried away, though. I wanted to proceed with caution.

"I hate to bring this up again," I said. "But are you really sure you're ready for a relationship?"

Scott didn't answer. He kissed me instead.

By this time, it was getting late, and I needed to start dressing for the formal. Scott told me he had something to do in the kitchen, and to please not come in. I was having trouble fixing my hair, but he came to take a look and said it looked beautiful and to leave it as it was. "As long as you feel that way," I said, moved. "That's all that matters."

He went back to the kitchen and returned a short time later with something behind his back.

"What are you hiding there?" I asked.

He showed me, and I almost couldn't believe it. "Is that a Pink Lady caramel apple?" I asked.

"It's my first attempt," he said. "I hope you like it." He'd rigged up a double-boiler and unwrapped the individual caramels and made it from scratch, the way it was supposed to be done. It was such a generous thing to do, yet he acted as if it was nothing. I was really moved by his thoughtfulness.

We shared the Pink Lady, and Scott opened one of the bottles of champagne. He was in his rented tux, and I was in a red, strapless evening gown, and I thought we looked nice. "There's going to be a lot of people I know at this fund-raiser," I said. "How should I introduce you?"

"I don't know."

"Well, are you seeing anyone else?"

"I'm not seeing anyone else. You're the only one I call 'sweetheart.' I'm completely monogamous."

"So would I be safe to call you my boyfriend?"

"I think that would be totally appropriate. Don't you?"

"Yes," I said, smiling. I felt good about this. I guess I was looking for clarification, and he had provided it. The relationship seemed to be moving along but I didn't want to be presumptuous. I smiled at him. "That makes everything a lot easier," I said.

We were supposed to pick up Saki, but she was running late, so we went to Casanova's, a local restaurant, for champagne and appetizers. Then we went to get Saki and returned to the restaurant. At one point, she and I disappeared into the rest room, and I told her about the rose petals and the caramel apple. "He's really cute," she said, but she didn't gush or anything. I got the feeling she was being cautious, or that maybe she saw something in him that I didn't see.

39

When we got back to the table, Scott was grinning and acting all full of himself. "Thank goodness you're back," he said. "While you girls were gone, the waiter was hitting on me."

"He was not!" I said.

"Was too," he insisted, pointing out the waiter in question.

"Did it bother you?" I asked.

"No," he said. "It's totally flattering when another guy finds you attractive."

I thought that was a little odd.

We left and stopped to pick up some film for Saki's camera, then drove over to the formal at the World Sports Café, in northeast Fresno. There was a full bar and people were dancing and the music was loud, and at one point Scott went outside to make a call on his cell phone. When I went to look for him later, he was handing out my new business card and telling everyone I was the best massage therapist in town.

One other thing I remember about that night is how strange it felt to describe Scott as my boyfriend. Even as the word tripped off my tongue—*boyfriend*—it was hard to get used to. It had been a very long time since I'd had an actual boyfriend. So, yes—it was strange, but it certainly felt good.

We had a couple of drinks and danced a little, though it was hard to dance in that dress, and later Scott had a cigar. He loved cigars and had his own cigar cutter. Finally we called it a night and went back to Saki's place. She had left her camera in his truck, and she wanted to take some pictures, so we went inside and posed and had a little fun. Saki and I were a bit tipsy, and we were laughing so hard that at one point we actually fell to the ground. We had a great time taking those pictures. My favorite was the one of Scott and me in front of Saki's Christmas tree.

It was a wonderful evening. When we returned to my place, Scott and I got careless and were intimate without protection. Scott apologized, and before I knew it we were having our first serious conversation about children. I told him I had tried birth control pills, but that they didn't agree with me. He said I shouldn't worry and announced that he'd been thinking about having a vasectomy.

I was pretty surprised by this. "Scott, you're so young. That's a pretty radical decision. Don't you want a child of your own?"

"No," he replied. "I don't really feel I need a biological child. Assuming that you and I are together, the one child I could see in my life would be Ayiana, and I would raise her as my own."

That bothered me on two fronts. First, I didn't understand how Scott, at age thirty, could be so certain he *didn't* want children. That was a pretty big decision, and potentially irreversible. Part of me assumed that maybe Scott hadn't met the right woman, but I didn't tell him so. The other reason it troubled me is that I definitely wanted more children. I shared this with Scott. I told him that I wanted to experience pregnancy in a joyous manner, with someone I loved. This was not something I had experienced with Ayiana. There had been no one there to share the joy of listening to my baby's heartbeat for the first time, no one next to me as the baby kicked away, no man at my side for those first sonograms. Still, I got beyond that soon enough. I loved being pregnant. I had a "textbook" pregnancy. Everything went flawlessly. And when Ayiana finally arrived, she changed my world forever. My life began anew. She was my little blessing; a gift from God.

Scott brought his face close to mine and studied me with great tenderness. "You are beautiful, Amber," he said. "And when I say you're beautiful, I'm talking about the inside, too."

Early that morning, Scott went off to get ready for a business trip to New Mexico and Arizona. That's what he told me, anyway. The fact is, he was going home to his wife, Laci. He was supposed to cook dinner for Laci and her mother, Sharon Rocha, and for Sharon's husband, Ron Grantski. I didn't know who these people were, nor that they even existed, but I'd know about them before long.

On December 16, Scott left a message on my

answering machine: "Hey sweetheart, Scott here. . . . I'm driving to the gym to do my weekly five-minute workout. I'll try to give you a call tomorrow."

I loved the sound of his voice and I played the message over several times. It was so sweet. There was something wonderful and heartening about my businessman boyfriend calling to check in, to let me know what he was up to. I began to think that Scott and I might actually have a real future together, and when I sat down to finish my Christmas cards I decided to enclose the picture of Scott and me. It was the one we had taken at Saki's house, right after the party. I wanted everyone to know about Scott. I wasn't going to hold back.

I didn't hear from Scott again till December 19, when he said he was calling from New Mexico. On December 20, we spoke only very briefly, and Scott said he'd call back. I didn't hear from him—apparently he wasn't out of town at all, but busy buying fishing lures, a rod, a reel, and a fishing license—and when he finally called, on December 21, I was relieved to hear his voice. "I really like to hear from you," I said. "You know how much I miss you."

"I'm sorry," he said. "I don't think my cell phone works too well in New Mexico. But I'll be back in Sacramento tomorrow and we can talk then."

He called the next day to say he was in Sacramento, and that he would be leaving for Maine soon. "Then I'm off to Europe."

"I miss you already," I said.

"Me too," he said.

He was going to be gone for almost a month, and—much as I hated birth control pills—this was the right time to start taking them. Scott told me not to bother. He knew I didn't respond well to the pill, and he again mentioned this business about a vasectomy. "Ayiana is enough for me," he said, echoing his earlier remark. "I would raise her as my own."

At that point, I began to get choked up. "This is such a big step," I said. "We need to discuss it."

"You're right," Scott said. "Why don't we talk about this when I get back? Maybe we can see a doctor together?" I thought this was both generous and thoughtful: here was a man who was willing to look at things from my point of view, not simply dismiss them out of hand.

I then asked how I could get in touch with him while he was gone. "I'm getting a P.O. box in Modesto."

"What good does that do? How will they get my mail to you?"

"It's sort of like a courier service," he explained. "I let them know where I am, and they can ship things to me like practically overnight."

This didn't sound right to me. Why would a

man who lived in Sacramento get a post office box in Modesto? But I let it slide. What did I know about courier services and overseas mail delivery? Not much, clearly. And my goal was to be able to get in touch with him. I had two Christmas gifts for him. One was a glass ornament with our photograph inside. I'd decorated it with gold foil and the words, *Merry Christmas 2002*. The whole thing was wrapped in blue foil and I'd enclosed a note: "To my love, from your love." It was sitting on my kitchen counter, ready for mailing. The other gift was a black chenille scarf, which I was crocheting myself, but wasn't quite done.

"I'll call you tomorrow," he said.

When I got off the phone, I realized that he never said he loved me. Not in person and not on the phone. Then again, I had never told him I loved him, either. Did I love him? I wasn't sure, though I felt I was certainly moving in that direction. And he cared for me—I could feel that. The way he treated me, the way he treated my daughter. He was a tender, caring person. I figured we were both being cautious, but that was as it should be: Good things take time.

....

*"Please God, tell me it's not the
same Scott Peterson."*

On December 23, true to his word, Scott called to tell me he was in Maine, with his father. I could hear the turn signal in the car, clicking away, but it seemed almost too quiet. I didn't have time to talk, though. I had to get to work. One of my regular clients came in for a massage later that day, and of course I was talking about Scott. She was curious about how his wife had died.

"Was it a slow death? An illness?"

"I don't know," I said.

"You need to know so you can understand what he went through," she said. "If he watched her die, that's one thing. If it was instant, that's another. You have to get into his head to see how he was affected, mentally."

I didn't disagree with her, but I didn't know when I was going to be able to broach the subject.

Another person who was curious about Scott was my good friend Richard Byrd, a Fresno police officer. He must have felt Scott sounded a little too good to be true, because he jokingly offered to check him out. I didn't take him seriously, of course, though by this time I was beginning to have some doubts of my own.

In the days that followed, the doubts kept gnawing away at me. One of the things that struck me was that I could often hear water in the background when Scott called. Thinking back on it, I realized this had happened even before he'd left for Maine. On one occasion he told me he was at home in Sacramento, in his hot tub. "I had to streak naked across the yard to get to the phone," he said. A couple of days after that, I again heard the unmistakable sound of running water. "Are you calling me from the shower or something?" I ventured.

"Yes," he said. "You caught me. I'm in the tub."

"How come?" I asked.

"I don't know," he said. "It just seems appropriate. I'm at my most comfortable and relaxed around water."

"Oh," I said.

"Tomorrow's Christmas Eve," he said, not that I needed him to remind me. "I'll call you."

The following morning, I woke up at sunrise, shaking and terrified. I had just had a horrible nightmare, which was rare for me, and it was doubly rare because it was so incredibly vivid. I will remember it as long as I live.

In the nightmare, a man with brown hair, with his back turned to me, was tickling Ayiana. I couldn't see his face, just as I couldn't quite see Ayiana, but I knew beyond a shadow of a doubt that it was my daughter. She was laughing gleefully, but the man became rougher and rougher, and before long Ayiana was having trouble breathing.

"Stop it," I shouted. "She can't breathe! She can't breathe!"

I tried to run to Ayiana's side, but my feet felt as if they were glued to the ground. Much as I struggled, I simply couldn't move. I kept screaming at the man—"Stop! Please stop!"—but he ignored me. Suddenly, another image flooded into my mind: I saw the face of a woman I didn't know. She had a broad, bright smile and curly, brown hair, and she was laughing hysterically. "Don't laugh!" I yelled at her. "Don't laugh! Can't you see he's smothering her?! Stop laughing! Stop!"

At that moment, I woke up, gasping for air. I was shaking. I don't believe I have ever felt that kind of fear in my life. Weeks later, however, when I saw an old photograph of Laci—Laci with long, permed hair—I felt that same intense fear all over again: Laci Peterson was the laughing woman in my dream.

This was early in the morning, December 24, 2002. Scott was supposed to be in Maine, duck-hunting, but he was nowhere near Maine. That was the day he went to the Berkeley Marina, in

San Francisco Bay, and paid five dollars for a permit to launch his new boat.

At around noon, while I was still recovering from the nightmare, my neighbors came over to find that I was still in my pajamas. We visited for a while—I fought the urge to tell them about the terrifying nightmare—and were interrupted by a call from my friend Richard Byrd, the Fresno police officer. He invited me to a party at the home of a mutual friend, a man who had a granddaughter Ayiana's age. "We need Ayiana there," he said, then added, laughing: "But I guess you can come too!"

Ayiana and I went to the party, and I again told Richard that I was beginning to wonder about Scott. But there was too much going on, and this wasn't the place to discuss it. At around six o'clock that very evening, while we were in the middle of festivities, Scott called the police to report his wife missing.

After the party, I drove home and put Ayiana to bed. Christmas Eve was almost over and Scott hadn't called. I felt lonely. I knew it was late on the East Coast—I still knew nothing of his lies— and I didn't want to risk waking him. So I sat down and began writing him a letter: "Dear Scott, Ayiana's asleep now. It's 10:28 p.m. and everything is ready for tomorrow. . . . I already miss you. You didn't call like you said you would. I just hope you're having a good time with your family. Did I mention that I miss you?"

I guess I was feeling needy. It was Christmas. I was lonely. "It's hard for me to believe that I'm not going to be seeing you for another five weeks," I went on. "I am happy for you that you've got to spend time w/ your brother and dad and uncle for Thanksgiving, and now your mom and dad for Christmas . . . (but) I wish you were spending these times with me, too."

I complained that he was always rushing off and that sometimes he even seemed to be in a hurry to get off the phone, and I told him that life would be a lot easier if I didn't care for him. "That would certainly hurt less!" I wrote. Then I signed off: "Working on loving you. Amber."

When I reread the letter, I was glad I'd written it, glad to have dealt with my feelings, but I wasn't sure I would ever mail it.

On Christmas morning, I spoke with Scott, but only briefly. He said he was relaxing with the family and had just gone on a hike. He described the Maine countryside, painting a vivid picture of trees heavy with snow, and told me about a white rabbit that had hopped across his path. "I need to go now," he said abruptly. "I'll call you later." Scott was never specific about when he would call, and I simply had to accept that.

Later that day, Ayiana and I went to celebrate

Christmas with Shawn and our close friends Paul and Lauren Benson at their home in Centerville. I had my cell phone with me, and Scott hadn't called, and I was upset. When Paul asked me what was wrong, I told him. He took my cell phone and asked for Scott's number and dialed it and left a message: "Scott, this is Paul Benson, a friend of Amber's. You don't promise a young lady that you're going to call and then fail to keep your promise."

I went over to talk to Shawn and told her that I really liked Scott. "I want so much for him to be the one," I said. "I want to give him my heart."

"It isn't time yet," Shawn said. "He lied to you. I know you understand why he lied, but take it easy. Give it time."

She was right and I knew she was right. I had given Scott my body, but—much as I wanted to—I still hadn't given him my heart. Now that I was beginning to have some doubts about him, I wondered whether I ever would.

Ten minutes later, my cell phone rang. It was Scott. I walked into another room, to talk to him privately, and at one point, I heard a woman's voice call his name. He said it was his mother, and I wanted to believe him—I had no reason not to—but for a moment I had my doubts. What if he wasn't with his mother? Had he told me his mother was going to Maine, too? I didn't know at the time that he'd been lying about Maine, and probably about everything else. Scott was home on Christmas Day, in Modesto, dealing with his missing wife. Even as we spoke, police and water rescue crews were in the Dry Creek area, near his property, searching the park and the surrounding water for his wife, Laci. At the end of the day, when their search failed to turn up any clues, they set up a Tip Line and put out the word: Any information about the disappearance of Laci Peterson could be phoned in anonymously.

I didn't know anything about this, of course. I don't even remember seeing any mention of the story on the news. I was busy with family and friends. One would think Scott had plenty to keep him busy, too, but here we were on the phone again, talking away, and he was his usual, charming self. I told him about Ayiana and how much she liked to sing, and I sang one of her favorite songs for him over the phone. It's called "Five Little Ducks Went Out to Play."

"I love it," he said when I'd finished. "The next time I see you, I want that song to be the first thing I hear."

That next day, December 26, a gift arrived from Scott, for Ayiana. I believe it was called a sky-gazer. I found batteries for it and turned it on. It projected stars onto the walls and ceiling. It reminded me of our hike to Squaw's Leap and of the way we'd cuddled in the cab of his truck, with Ayiana, and watched the stars come out. Ayiana loved the sky-gazer, too. She couldn't get enough of it.

Later, when I went to get rid of the box, I noticed that the shipper had listed an address for Scott on Emerald Street, in Modesto. I couldn't understand that. Surely it was a mistake. I tried to call Scott, but I couldn't get through, and when we finally connected, I tried not to act all suspicious. I thought it was just me—that my insecurities were showing.

"Ayiana loved the toy," I said.

"Did you see the note?"

"No. What note? I just saw the invoice."

"Invoice?" he said, sounding suddenly upset. "There's not supposed to be an invoice. Just a note."

I went to look for the invoice and I saw a tiny little note near the bottom, typed in letters almost too small to read. It was in Spanish, and Scott translated it for me. I think it said, "To my girls . . . The angels are watching over you. Where's the first star in the sky?"

I was very touched. I remember getting a little mad at myself for having entertained even the smallest doubts about Scott.

He then asked me if I'd had fun on Christmas Day.

"Uh huh," I said. "I was at the Bensons'. I

can't wait for you to meet them. You're really going to like them."

"I sort of met Paul on the phone," he said. "He left me a voicemail. I like the fact that he's watching out for you."

While we were on the phone, chatting about things of little importance, a volunteer center was just opening at the Red Lion Hotel, near Scott's home. Laci's friends and family had established a $100,000 reward for information leading to her safe return.

The next day, police found a single hair in a pair of pliers at the bottom of Scott's boat. Scott, meanwhile, was once again on the phone with me, telling me he was heading to New York and would then be flying to Europe.

I remember asking him if he was always going to be traveling this extensively. "No," he said. "In fact, that's one of the reasons I'm going to Europe. I'm going to renegotiate my contract. I'm sick of traveling so much. I've had enough traveling."

I phoned later, wanting to leave a message, wanting him to hear my friendly voice when he checked his messages from Europe, and was surprised when he answered. "Wow," I said. "I thought you'd be in the air, on your way to Paris."

"Hello?" he said. "Hello?"

Then the line went dead. It rang a moment later. "Amber, it's me. Hi."

"Hey. Where are you?"

"In New York."

"New York?"

"Yeah," he said. "My flight was delayed, and I missed the 8:30."

"From this morning? Why didn't you call me?"

"I don't know. I was just wandering around, checking things out, thinking about things."

"Were you thinking about me?"

"What's wrong, Amber?"

"I don't know," I said, but I knew—and it upset me. I was being mistrustful, and it was wrong. "I'm sorry," I said. "I have this thing about trust. It's not you. It's me."

"You don't have to apologize for that," he said. "I should have called. I should have been more understanding. I wasn't being sensitive to your needs."

For some reason, I felt very close to tears. I reminded him of our conversation on the night before the formal, and how I'd asked if he was my boyfriend. "Do you remember what you said? 'There is no one else, sweetheart. It's you and me exclusively.' Do you remember that?" All sorts of crazy thoughts were running through my head. He was so thoughtful, so kind. He had told me he was monogamous. Why was I doing this?

Why was I bent on destroying such a promising relationship?

"Of course I remember," he said. "And nothing has changed. On the contrary, we're stronger than ever. We have a future together, Amber. And I'm not going to do anything to mess it up."

I thanked him for being so understanding, and I told him it went beyond the trust issues. "It's hard," I explained. "I've spent so many holidays alone."

"Next year will be different, Amber. You and I will be spending a lot of holidays together."

Hearing that made me feel a little better. "So you're off to Europe," I said, missing him already. "How long will you be gone?"

"I don't know exactly," he said. "Let me give you that P.O. box in Modesto," he said, and then he gave me the address. "I'll write you, too," he added. "The phones are really bad in Europe." He had given me another cell number, one that he thought would work better overseas, and he wanted to make sure I still had it. Then he told me he needed to get off the phone. He was going to have dinner and get a massage. "The airlines gave me a hundred-dollar coupon," he said.

"A coupon for a massage?" I asked. This was hard to believe. Much later I learned that massages were being offered to the volunteers at the

Red Lion, in Modesto, so obviously massages were on his mind.

"I have to go," he said. "I'll call you back at seven."

This struck me as unusual. Scott never gave me an exact time when he'd call.

He called at seven o'clock sharp. We had a terrible connection. I was at the home of my friend Denise, and I asked him to call me there, on the land line. But he said no—his flight was boarding—and he had to run.

"Have a safe flight," I said, and he said goodbye and hung up.

I turned to look at Denise. "That's so strange," I said. "Why does he never talk to me on a land line? And why would he suggest calling me at seven if that was when his flight was boarding?"

I had known Denise forever, since high school, and in fact I met Shawn through Denise. And the more I told her about Scott, the more I realized I was beginning to have serious misgivings about him. I didn't go into a lot of detail, but I was thinking about a number of things. The constant travel. The Modesto address on the gift receipt. That business about the local P.O. box. Mostly, though, I guess I was bothered by those calls from the shower, and by that woman in the background, calling his name. Was he hiding in the bathroom from someone? And who could that someone be?

Something was wrong here. Feminine intuition had been telling me for weeks that I should watch my step with Scott Peterson, but I'd been so in love with the idea of him—of this perfect man, of our perfect romance—that I refused to hear it.

Denise was very good with computers, so I asked her to help me run a search on Scott. The search turned up dozens of Scott Lee Petersons across the country, and a handful of them quite close to home. There were several Scott Lee Petersons in Modesto, for example, but we didn't get anything on the one we were looking for. We tried TradeCorp, where he worked, and nothing came up. We tried the Rotary Club and had no luck there, either. We looked in Sacramento, where he said he lived, and we checked out the San Luis Obispo area, where he once told me he'd gone to school.

A few of the names we dug up sounded like they might possibly be him, so we made some calls. The first Scott Lee Peterson didn't sound right, but I told him I thought I had done business with him. He said I was mistaken and I apologized and got off the phone. Another one was married and had four kids and sounded much older. The third Scott Peterson wondered if I was in fact looking for the Scott Peterson who owned a restaurant. That rang a faint bell, but I didn't recall whether Scott had said anything about a restaurant, and I said no and thanked him and hung up.

Hard as it is to believe, especially when you consider the fact that Scott Peterson's wife was missing, we came up completely empty-handed. Maybe it was too soon; maybe the story about Laci hadn't yet made it beyond the Modesto area.

When I got home that night, none the wiser for my efforts, I called my friend Richard Byrd, the police officer. He wasn't home, so I left a message on his answering machine, asking him to call me. I didn't go into detail.

On Sunday, I went to church and asked God for His help. I did a prayer request. This is where you take a slip of paper and write down exactly what it is you want, and you leave the paper in a box at the church. In my request, I said that I had a lot of mistrust in me because I'd had a great deal of heartbreak in my life, and that I didn't like being so mistrustful. I said I wanted to feel trust in my heart so that my relationships would stop being such a struggle. I asked God to open my eyes and ears, to let me see and hear whatever it was I needed to see and hear, and to help me get on with my life, especially the relationship part of my life. Then I folded the slip of paper and put it inside the box.

I needed to get clear on this. If there was something about Scott I should know, I wanted to know it. And if it was just me—me and my trust issues—I wanted to know that, too.

After church, I went to Rite Aid to drop off my Christmas film, and I left it there, and I tried my friend Richard again to tell him I was down the street from his place. He wasn't home, so I took Ayiana and we got in my car and my cell phone rang. It was Richard. He said he had just got home, and that his roommate was there, too, and that I was welcome to stop by. I drove over and we visited for a while, and I told Richard and his roommate about Scott. He knew I had some misgivings about him, but he also knew how much I liked him. "Whenever he calls me 'sweetie,'" I said, "I just melt."

"You know why he calls you 'sweetie'?" Richard said. "It's because he doesn't want to get your name wrong. He doesn't want to confuse you with all of his other sweeties."

"Great!" I said, sarcastically. "Thanks a lot!"

But I could see Richard wasn't kidding around. He and his roommate had a lot of questions about Scott. They wanted me to describe him in detail. They wanted to know how old he was and where he lived and what kind of vehicle he drove. I told them everything, including the fact that he'd lost his wife, and they said they'd make some calls and nose around.

That night, Scott called me twice and I missed both his calls. I called him back but couldn't reach him. The following night, December 29, I was at another party at the Bensons, chatting with Paul. I was telling him all about Scott, *again*, when my cell phone rang.

It was Richard. He said he'd found an article about Scott Peterson on the Internet. This Scott Peterson lived in Modesto, and his wife was missing. "I'm not sure it's your Scott Peterson," he said, sounding casual.

"How could that be my Scott Peterson?" I replied. My Scott Peterson was single and lived alone in a big 1940s house in Sacramento. I just knew he had to be wrong. After all, as I reminded him, I had searched the Internet myself, with my friend Denise, and we'd turned up many Scott Lee Petersons, but not mine. Still, it's not as if I didn't have my doubts. "Keep looking," I suggested. "If you find out anything for sure, call me. I don't care how late it is."

"Okay," he said.

I went back to join the party.

At 1:40 a.m., my cell phone rang. It was Richard again. This time, he didn't sound so casual. On the contrary, there was a frightening intensity in his voice.

"Amber," he said. "You're not going to like this; I'm not even sure I should be telling you this."

"What?"

"That man you told me about, Scott Peterson—it sounds like the same Scott Peterson from Modesto."

"What Scott Peterson?"

"He's married, and his wife is missing, and there's been a huge search under way since last week."

I was in shock. "W-what do you mean his wife is missing?" I said.

I didn't want to believe it. I closed my eyes and prayed: "Please God, tell me it's not the same Scott Peterson."

"We have been praying for someone
like you to come forward."

Richard was suddenly all business. He told me that Scott's wife had been missing for more than a week, and that he was pretty sure it was the same Scott. "He fits your description," he said.

"Oh my God."

"Amber," he said. "I'm going to give you the number for the Modesto police. You need to call them right away."

The moment I got off the phone with Richard, I called the Modesto Police Department. It was 1:43 a.m., the morning of December 30, and the party was slowly winding down. I told the woman who answered that I might have some information about Scott Peterson. There was a lot of back and forth, and she asked me what I knew, and I said that before I told her anything I wanted to make sure I had the right Scott Peterson, and that it would help if at the very least she could confirm his date of birth. It took about twenty minutes of talking and being put on hold and more talking, but finally she came back on the line and confirmed Scott's date of birth.

My heart sank, and I felt winded. I could

hardly breathe. The Scott I knew, or thought I knew, was supposed to be in Paris, or en route to Paris. But this Scott, the other Scott, perhaps the *real* Scott, was in Modesto, searching for his wife Laci, who was eight months pregnant.

"Let me take down your information," the woman said. She seemed very nonchalant about the whole thing.

"You don't understand," I said. "I've been dating this guy. He's supposed to be on his way to Europe, and now I'm finding out that he's here and he has a pregnant wife and that she's missing?!"

"If you give me your name and number," she said in a dull monotone, "one of the officers will get back to you."

Still in shock, I gave her my name and number. When I came out of the room, I was sobbing. I don't remember how long I was sobbing. Shawn and Paul hurried to my side.

"What's wrong?" Shawn asked. "You're as white as a ghost."

"I, I, I—" I couldn't seem to make my mind work. I couldn't get the words out.

"Amber," Paul said firmly. "What's going on?"

"It's him," I said, still shaking and crying. "It's the same Scott Peterson. Up in Modesto, the one with the pregnant, missing wife. That's the guy I've been dating." I was having trouble breathing.

The next thing I knew, Richard showed up at the Bensons'. He brought a couple of newspaper articles and I had a look, and one of the first things I saw was a photograph of Scott's truck. The article described Scott as a fertilizer salesman, and even mentioned that he was a member of the Rotary Club. Now there could be no doubt. "I can't believe this is happening to me," I said.

I looked over at Shawn. I think she was crying. She felt awful. She kept apologizing, saying how badly she felt for having set me up with him. She couldn't believe this was happening, either. It was as if both of us were in the same nightmare.

I stayed all night at the Bensons', but I couldn't sleep. I kept going over everything in my mind. That first meeting at the Elephant Bar. Dinner. The karaoke bar. I had let this man pick my daughter up at preschool. I had been intimate with him too quickly. I had shared my fears and my hopes and dreams with him, and he had all but promised that we had an amazing future ahead of us. I remembered the cork with our names on it, along with the date, and I remembered thinking that it was going to be the first of many.

I couldn't stop my mind from racing. The images kept coming, tumbling toward me. The hike to Squaw's Leap. The pop-up book. The three dozen roses. My Pink Lady caramel apple.

71

I don't think I slept more than an hour or two, and I only slept then because I was so overwhelmed that my mind and body simply shut down.

Early the next morning, Shawn tiptoed into my room to tell me that there was something on the news. I went to have a look, but the TV was grainy and it was hard to make out much detail. There was some footage of several members of Laci Peterson's family, crying and asking for the public's help, but no sign of Scott.

Paul then tried his luck on the Internet. He found a number of articles, and something about a recent break-in at a house in the Peterson's neighborhood, but nothing much about Scott, the husband. "Look," Paul said, showing me Laci's website—a site I was to become very familiar with in the weeks and months ahead. "People all over the country are writing in to send prayers to the family."

I called the police again, and I got another dispatcher. I know I was a little irritated by this time, because I had some information, and I wanted to help, and I thought they should have called me back by now. I began to repeat what I'd told the first dispatcher, when suddenly she put me on hold.

A moment later, a man took the phone. "This is Detective Al Brocchini," he said. "I want to thank you for calling us back."

"I don't understand why nobody's called me," I said.

"Well, that was an oversight. We'd like to talk to you. Can we come see you?"

"When?"

"When are you available?"

We agreed to meet at eleven, at my place, and I gave them my address. Shawn drove me back and we ended up waiting outside because I was a little spooked. I didn't want to go into my own home. I kept thinking, *I can't believe this. This isn't really happening. I'm in the middle of a bad dream and I know I'm going to wake up soon.*

At eleven o'clock, two officers showed up in an unmarked sedan. One of them was Al Brocchini. The other was Jon Buehler. They identified themselves and showed us their badges and we went inside. It was surreal.

"It's the strangest thing," I said. "I went to church, and I prayed for God to open my eyes, and He did. He showed me. God made it so I could witness the truth."

And Jon Buehler said, "We have been praying for someone like you to come forward."

"Maybe God has brought us together," I said.

Then he asked if he could record our conversation, and I said I didn't see why not, and he set up the small tape recorder and the microphone. When they were ready, Shawn told her side of the story first. How she met Scott in Anaheim.

That he seemed like a nice guy. That she'd thought of me because I was looking to settle down with someone who was serious about the future.

When she was done, it was my turn, and I found myself asking Shawn if she minded stepping into the other room. I guess I knew that some of the details were going to be embarrassing, and this was difficult enough already. Shawn was very understanding. The moment she left the room, I plunged in:

> "First time I heard about him I can give you a date—well, it was early November. Shawn had told me about this guy she met and she uh, he was just absolutely wonderful and (she) thought highly of him, she said . . . she thinks highly of me and thought that we would, you know, be a good match. . . ."

I told them about the first time Scott called, and about our meeting at the Elephant Bar. I told them about dinner at the private room in the Japanese restaurant, and—much as it shamed me—about spending that first night with him at his room at the Radisson Hotel. I told them about the day he met Ayiana, and about shopping for the Christmas tree, and about our hike, and about sitting in the cab of his truck, looking at the stars. And I told them about all the wonderful dates that followed, and how excited I was about the future. And then I told them about the afternoon he told me that he had lost his wife, which was precipitated by Shawn's discovery that he had lied to us both.

This, too, is from the police report:

> ". . . so I asked him, I said, you know, when you came to me later about being married . . . I didn't know Shawn is the reason you came to me on the 9th. I said . . . When were you going to come to me with this? And he said, well, I was going to come to you after I came back from Europe, was going to see . . . where things were going to go with us . . . but, you know, then (Shawn) confronted me. And I said . . . that just—that does bother me. And he goes, Amber, . . . I know, I'm sorry, but that was . . . it was wrong. He goes, Amber I just . . . I know you're an independent woman and . . . and I just hope that you can trust me enough that—in a decision that would affect you and Ayiana—that you would be able to say yes, and trust me in that. And I said, I said . . . Can I trust you with my heart?"

I felt oddly detached from the story, as if that wasn't really me, sitting there, talking to the police about a man who might possibly have murdered his wife. No one had said anything about murder, of course, because no one had to: everyone was thinking it.

From time to time, however, as I continued talking, I would listen to myself, sitting there sharing intimate details about my relationship with Scott with two men I'd only just met—details so intimate I didn't want my best friend to hear them—and it was just completely overwhelming. I had trusted Scott Peterson, I had almost given him my heart, and he had been lying to me from the start. And the lies never stopped. His wife was missing—and eight months pregnant—and Scott had been on the phone with me almost every day. He had been talking about his *feelings* for me, and about our *future*, and about that big lonely house in Sacramento that was just waiting for the right woman.

My God! He was married. He hadn't lost his wife. He still had a wife. And there was a child on the way.

I kept thinking, *I have to do everything I can to help these police officers. I have to help them find Laci and her baby.*

When the interview was finally over, and the tape recorder was turned off, I was still desperate to help. "I have pictures of me and Scott," I said. "I have presents from him. I even have a book he gave my little girl."

They were eager to see everything, determined to be as thorough as possible. They took several books from my shelves because Scott had handled them. They took Ayiana's pop-up book. They took scrapings from the bottom of the shoes Ayiana had worn on the hike. They took an empty wine bottle. They took the wine cork with our names on it. And they took the skygazer and the invoice with the Modesto address. In a trash can that hadn't been emptied for a while I found a condom wrapper, and I gave them the unopened condoms that Scott had left at my place the last time he had spent the night. I gave them all the pictures of Scott and me, including the ones Saki had taken at her place. And when I told them about the film I'd dropped off at Rite Aid, they asked if I would call them before I went to pick it up so that they could take that as evidence, too.

Finally, they took the Christmas gift I'd been making for Scott: the glass ornament with our photograph in the middle. I had written a card to go with it. It said, "To my love from your love." The gift was wrapped and ready to mail, but it would never get mailed.

It was strange. I was happy to give them all of these things. I wanted to give them anything that was even remotely connected to Scott. In retrospect, I realize that I wanted to do more than help; I wanted to purge Scott from my heart and home.

Jon Buehler told me again how much he appreciated my courage. "I mean it," he said again. "We were praying for someone like you to come forward."

Someone like you. I repeated the words in my head. *Someone like you.*

It made me wonder who that someone was.

I was born in Los Angeles on February 10, 1975, the second of two girls. My sister, Ava, is three years older than me. My parents, Ron and Brenda Frey, moved to the Fresno area when we were still very young, and the marriage fell apart when I was four.

For a while we were shunted between the two homes, and it seemed as if both our parents wanted to be parents. They tried hard to make things work, but it was clear from the start that they weren't going to be the best of friends. It made me realize, even in my youth, that there are two sides to every story. I remember my mother loading up the car the day we left, and telling us to get ready, that it was time to go, and how I went back into the house to confront my father and stomped on his foot. "I hate you!" I said. But of course I didn't mean it. Years later, I realized I was simply acting out my mother's feelings, and that those feelings would change over time—that this was the nature of feelings.

For a while we lived with my mother, in a modest apartment complex. She worked at a local hospital, in some kind of nursing capacity, and had a second job as a waitress, and she was seldom home. But I was a good kid, and I didn't need much parenting, so it wasn't an issue.

When Mom wasn't working, she was often out on the town, hoping to meet someone new. My father would come to visit from time to time, and it always made me happy. He was a handsome man, in a cowboy hat, and I was glad to see that I didn't hate him after all.

One day, my mother met another man, and we moved to a nice house in Fresno. He was a good guy, and from time to time he'd take us camping, and life went along without much incident. On Sundays, my sister and I would go to the Baptist church. They used to send a bus around for anyone who needed transportation, and the springs in the seats were so taut that we'd bounce and hit our heads every time we went over a bump. I loved it. Mom didn't go to church with us. She had gone once, and she had dressed casually, and she felt as if the other women hadn't approved. Right or wrong, she never went back.

Her relationship ended after a few years, kind

of abruptly, and we packed up and moved to a different apartment complex. Before long, my mother fell in love with the father of Ava's best friend, and the next thing I knew they were married and I had a stepsister. Ava and my new stepsister were in the same class, and they often excluded me from their activities. But that marriage didn't last long, and my new stepfather and new stepsister faded into memory.

The following year, shortly after I turned nine, my mother met Mike. They married and have been together ever since.

Soon after Mike came into the picture, however, we were sent to live with Dad, up in the mountains at Yosemite Springs Parkway. My father was happy to have us. He was living alone, and working as a self-employed contractor, and we filled the house with life.

"I always wanted you two," he said. "Your mother didn't let me see you as much as I wanted to."

I often went to work with him, especially on weekends. I helped build fences. I tarred roofs. I even laid brick. At other times, I went around the neighborhood, washing cars. It taught me the value of hard work.

My father had been seeing someone before we moved in, and he continued seeing her, and they eventually married. His wife was a little odd, and not much for family life. She was either in her room or down at the stables, and we hardly ever saw her, so when the marriage ended we didn't really miss her. Now it was just Dad and Ava and me again, a small, incomplete family.

All in all, though, it was a pleasant life. We were in the foothills, and I rode my bike everywhere and took long walks and went hiking through the mountains. There was a community pool nearby, and I would always find friendly faces there, and I felt as if I didn't want for anything in the world. There was also a church at the clubhouse, up near the pool, and my dad would take us there every Sunday. We'd whine about it, not wanting to go, but one Sunday a new pastor came to town, a man called Cody, and he started something called Friday Night Live. It was for older kids, and they would have Bible Study and play games like Ditch 'em—a version of hide-and-seek, only it's played at night, in the dark—and Cody let me tag along.

Every Friday, late in the afternoon, Cody would drive around in a VW bug, picking us up for Friday Night Live. He'd stop in front of each house and honk the horn, and we kids would come running out and pile in. Sometimes there were twelve of us scrunched into that tiny car, and we would laugh all the way to the clubhouse church.

I loved it. It was the one thing in my week that I most looked forward to. And because I was the youngest kid there, everyone was really nice to me.

Cody was a great storyteller. He had reddish hair, and pale skin, and one night he showed us a video about a young man who got in serious trouble with the law and ended up in jail. It turned out that that young man was Cody himself. He told us that he finally came to a point where he felt compelled to turn his life over to God, and from that day forward everything had changed for the better. I was only twelve at the time, and this made a big impression on me. I wasn't sure what it meant to turn your life over to God, but if God could take a man and turn him completely around, as He had done with Cody, it was surely a good and powerful testimony. I especially liked the fact that Cody wasn't ashamed to show us who he'd been, and that people could change their ways if they were willing to do the work.

One day, out of the blue, Mom and Mike came to visit, and she greeted us like she'd only been away for a long weekend, not for such a long time. She was living in Fresno, about forty-five minutes away, and soon we were visiting two or three times a month.

My grandmother was also in my life. From time to time, she would show up and take me to the People's Church, in Fresno. Every Easter, as they do at churches everywhere, they'd talk about the Crucifixion, and sometimes they'd show movies about the death and resurrection of Jesus. It was exciting, but I also found it a little scary. Once, after having heard that God knew everything about us, I hid out in the bathroom and wept. I knew I wasn't a perfect little girl, and I didn't know whether I ever would be perfect. Knowing that God could see everything, I worried about every little thought. If I didn't like some kid, for example, I suspected that God wouldn't approve, and that He might punish me in some small way. It was troubling, because I knew there was no hiding from Him, and because I didn't want to be bad—and I wasn't even sure what constituted "bad." In time, however, I came to accept the fact that He was a benevolent God, and this made my life much easier.

One other thing I remember clearly from those early years is the fact that I was very skinny. I was always being teased about this, and about the way I dressed because, admittedly, I was a bit of a ragamuffin. I lived mostly with my dad, and my mom never really took the time to show me how to dress, or how to try to look pretty, so I was kind of a mess. My sister, Ava, didn't help much, either. She was always mad at me, for reasons I never understood, but all of that changed in the summer of 1985, and I was sent to live with my mom.

I didn't understand it at all. Why did Ava get

to stay with Dad? I was crushed. I'd been taken away from my life and from my friends and from Cody, and for the longest time I didn't even get to see my father.

I was very unhappy at Mom's, with both her and Mike. It's not that they didn't try, but I was withdrawn and lost interest in everything.

One day, a letter arrived from my dad, and he said he was coming to see me. I was very excited, but the day he was supposed to show up my mom pulled me out of school and took me away. I guess she didn't want him to see me, and she didn't explain why. He later told me that he'd been writing fairly regularly, but the letters never reached my hands. He finally sent one to the school, and the school gave it to me, and he told me that he loved me very much and wanted desperately to see me.

Shortly thereafter, my parents got into a custody fight, and I was sent to a mediator and asked to choose between them. I was only twelve years old, and I thought it was a bit much to ask a child to make such a monumental decision—so I refused to do it. As a result, they chose for me. They sent me to live with my mom.

During my freshman year in high school, I met a senior boy who became my first real boyfriend. He was several years older than me, and very charming, and he was constantly pressuring me for intimacy. It was very strange: all my young life I had felt I would remain a virgin till I married, and suddenly, at age fifteen, I relented. I think I knew it was wrong, but I was convinced we were in love, and that that somehow made it less wrong. What did I know? I was still a child.

I was not a great student. I didn't apply myself, and no one at home ever bothered telling me to study, so my grades suffered. One of the few things I really enjoyed, however, was singing, so I joined the school choir. I had stopped going to church, but I found my way back there, and before long I remembered how much it had meant to me.

By the end of my junior year, my boyfriend and I had begun to drift apart. He was very jealous and very controlling, and he wouldn't let me wear certain things because he thought it made other boys look at me. He was constantly bossing me around and telling me what I could and couldn't do, and we were always arguing.

This spilled over into my home life, and my mom and I were in constant disagreement. I think it was simple adolescent angst, but it got out of hand, and one day I told her I couldn't live with her anymore and went back to my father's place. Ava had moved out by this time—she was married already, and had a child—so that wasn't a problem. And Dad was seeing a woman, but it was mostly casual, and she wasn't around much, either.

Sometimes my father's sister came to visit. I called her Aunt Nanny. She was a caring, loving woman, and genuinely curious about my life—she always had lots of questions for me—and she was also spiritual in a very unconventional way. She liked to read palms, for example. I remember one afternoon she looked at my palm and said, "Amber, you're going to be a massage therapist some day, and you're going to be very successful." I had a good laugh over that. I couldn't even imagine putting my hands on people's naked bodies.

That same year, I met a boy in school and really fell for him. We had an instant bond. His name was Moises, and he had long, dark hair and a mole on his nose, and I found him amazingly easy to talk to. The first time we talked on the phone, we talked for hours and hours. I guess we were a couple of lost souls. He had grown up in Santa Cruz, and his parents were ministers with the Salvation Army. They had just been transferred to the area, and this was his first year in Fresno.

Moises was a vegetarian, and I began to cut back on meat, and under his influence I became a bit of hippie. I grew my hair long and stopped shaving my legs and once again reverted to being a ragamuffin. Many years later, I ran into someone I'd known in those days, and she insisted that I'd been a real trendsetter. I was surprised to hear this, but when I thought back on it I realized that in some ways she was right. I guess I really did have my own fashion sense, though the word "fashion" probably wasn't part of my vocabulary. I guess I was just being myself—funky, crocheted hats, thrift shop dresses, etc.—but to some people I must have seemed stylish and chic. Of course, there were times when I was forced to "clean up real nice" for special occasions, and I'm not sure how stylish I looked then.

Moises and I were inseparable, and he was a good, calming influence. Under his guidance, I soon found myself attending church on a regular basis.

Before long, I moved back with my mom, and found myself at Clovis High School. I got a part-time job at the espresso bar of the local hospital, along with a second part-time job at Thrifty, the drugstore chain. The steady paychecks gave me some cash and a solid sense of self: I graduated from Clovis in 1993 with a 4.0 grade point average.

I went to Fresno City College. Moises went there too, studying art, and we continued to see each other for several years. I began to work with children, which had always been an interest of mine, and in 1997 I graduated with a degree in child development and another in general studies. I had done it on my own, and I was proud of myself. I was the first person in my immediate family to get a college degree. I had even saved $2,000 and paid cash for a car.

Proud as I was of these accomplishments, there was one thing that happened during my college years that still fills me with shame. I got careless, and I became pregnant. And I went off and did what so many girls my age did and continue to do to this day: I had an abortion.

I was in terrible emotional pain, but I didn't tell a soul. Not my family. Not my best friends. I thought that if I talked about it, it would make it real—and I desperately wanted for it to not be real. To help me cope, I turned again to God. I joined a local church and got a job there teaching Sunday school. After a time, they offered me a full-time job in their after-school program. These things kept me busy and made me feel somewhat better, but there was still a heaviness in my heart.

One day, our youth minister suggested I might be interested in an event that was coming to Fresno. She even bought me a ticket. It was a meeting of the Chosen Women, a group that's similar to Promise Keepers, but exclusively for women. It was an astonishing experience. Thousands of women attended, filling an entire football stadium, praying, singing, and giving witness. At one point, they asked anyone who'd had an abortion to please step forward, and hundreds of women got out of their seats and approached the stage. I was one of them. I closed my eyes and listened to the sea of sobbing women around me, and I was completely overwhelmed. I realized I wasn't alone. There was so much honesty there, and so much forgiveness that I, too, burst into tears.

After the meeting, the women mingled and prayed and talked about their experiences, and I felt such relief and acceptance that I repented to God. I had made a mistake, but it was not one I would ever repeat.

Ironically, the previous weekend I had met a young man at the gym, a man I'll call Steve. He was a pleasant person, in good shape, but he was having all sorts of personal troubles. He was married and his wife was pregnant, but they were no longer living together.

By this time, I had my own apartment, a good job, and a brand-new truck, and one night, feeling newly liberated, thanks largely to that afternoon with the Chosen Women, I went with some friends to listen to some reggae music at a local pub. I ran into Steve, and he asked if I wanted to go dancing, and he took me to a club. That was the night he told me he was a professional dancer.

Steve worked long hours, and I was working hard, too. I put in forty hours with the kids from Monday to Friday, went to the gym five days a week, and taught Sunday school every Sunday after church. Steve often went to church with me.

"I am a man of God," he told me shortly after we had met. This was not something I heard often, and it swayed me. Steve was also honest about his personal life, and I am a great admirer of honesty. He told me that he and his girlfriend had gone to Las Vegas, and that after a night of hard partying they had ended up in a drive-thru chapel, then checked into a hotel as man and wife. They returned to Fresno and soon discovered that she was pregnant, and they tried to make a go of it, though he said they both knew from the start that they had made a big mistake. Soon enough, the relationship was over, but Steve had a child on the way, and he told me that—when the time came—he intended to be a father to his child.

Then he admitted to me that he had been with another woman since the break-up with his wife, but that, too, had ended abruptly. He said that lately he had found himself wishing that his wife had had an abortion, so that he could start fresh. I told him it was a good thing she hadn't had the abortion, and that one day, soon, he would see that she had done the right thing. Then I told him about my own abortion, and how it had practically ruined my life, and it helped him to understand what I'd been saying, and to prepare him for what lay ahead.

One night he called to tell me that his pregnant wife had shown up at his apartment, screaming hysterically and causing a scene. "She was being real crazy," he said. "Getting in my face. And she's pregnant, so of course I had to be careful. If I even looked at her funny, she would have called the cops." He felt terrible about the whole thing, and he thanked me for being such a tremendous source of support during those trying times, and our friendship soon turned to romance. Before long, Steve told me he was in love with me. I was shocked, to be honest, but I cared for him, too, and we tried to make things work. Of course, there was another woman in his life, with a child on the way, and we were going to have to face up to it. I told him that this child was going to be in our lives, and that I would welcome the child, but I also said that I would understand if he wanted to go back to his wife. I didn't think there was much chance of that—they had done irreparable damage to their relationship—but I wanted him to know that it was an option, and that if things changed he should just be honest with me and do what needed to be done. I meant it, too. With all my heart. I told him I would support whatever decision he made.

"I'm never going back to my wife," he said. "That's never going to happen. I'm crazy about you and I want to be with you. And I appreciate the fact that you're going to help me with my child. I have seen you with children, and you're wonderful with them, and I really couldn't ask for more."

Steve moved in with me, and as the weeks turned into months the ex-wife became an increasing presence. As the day of her delivery got closer, I began to sense that Steve's feelings toward me were changing.

At one point, my friends and I decided to give Steve a baby shower. I wanted him to know that I had really meant what I said when I told him I would accept a future with this baby. That very day, his wife went into labor, and he went to the hospital to be with her. It was hard for me, but I remembered what I had said to him. I had meant it, and I wasn't going to be weak.

Steve was a good father, given the circumstances. For the next few months, he went to see the baby often. I dealt with it. I figured it was no different than having a relationship with a divorced man—a man who had other responsibilities—and that it didn't mean Steve loved me less. Still, I wanted to be sure that he was happy with his decision.

"Remember what we talked about?" I said. "That if your feelings change, and you need to go back and be a family with her and your son, I will understand." It wasn't easy to face up to this possibility, but I had God on my side, and I knew He would help me get through it if it came to that.

And Steve said, "No. You have nothing to worry about. I want to be with you. I'm very happy with you."

She wasn't happy with me, of course, and she made it known that she'd rip my eyes out if she got a chance. Even though I hadn't broken them apart—I hadn't come into Steve's life till long after their relationship had collapsed, and he'd even been with another woman after it ended—I understood how she felt, and I could see that she needed someone to blame. That's human nature, after all. We all find it hard to take responsibility for our own actions.

I tried to make the center hold, and I prayed for both of us, but I think Steve lost his way. His attitude changed. His behavior changed. Without going into detail, I will just say that he did some things that he shouldn't have done, and that—even though I forgave him in my heart—I knew we were drifting apart.

One day his wife called to ask me to please meet with her. I went. She told me that she didn't want Steve back, that all she wanted was her son, and she was hoping I might help her get sole custody. She knew that Steve and I were having serious problems, but I didn't want to get in the middle of a custody battle, and I told her so. Steve and I soon went our separate ways. Part of me believed he might think more clearly if I wasn't in his life, but another part of me—the more honest part—knew that we were finished.

I don't know what happened to them, or how the custody issues were resolved, or even if they were resolved, but I heard that within a year they were divorced and that Steve had gone back to Las Vegas and married someone else.

It had been a very trying relationship. I felt like a wreck, and I felt I didn't have enough energy for my job. I didn't think it was fair to the children at the school where I worked. So I quit and tried to focus on myself for a change. I took some simple jobs that were less emotionally demanding. I sold jewelry for a while. I worked for Airborne Express. I moved into an apartment in the Tower District, an artsy Fresno neighborhood. I would take long walks and talk with God and work on rebuilding myself, and I spent a great deal of time alone and found I was okay with that.

Then one afternoon, while I was having lunch at a little Mexican place, two guys at a nearby table started talking to me. One of them told me his name was Anthony. He said he was having a party that night, and invited me to come, and I took his address but never went. It's not that I didn't like him—he was certainly nice enough— but he was a complete stranger, and that wasn't my style.

A month later, right in that very neighborhood, I was getting out of my car and I saw him again. He remembered my name, and said he had missed me at his party. "All night long," he said, "I was waiting for my special guest."

Anthony asked me out, and I went, and I found him very charming and personable, as well as creative and ambitious. In some ways, he reminded me of Moises, who had been such a stabilizing force in my life. This was very appealing to me, especially after that roller-coaster ride with Steve. In no time at all, we were inseparable. I didn't know where our relationship was going, or where my future would take me, but I wanted to keep an open mind.

Unfortunately, my mind might have been a little *too* open. One day I saw an ad in the paper— a photographer was looking for female models—and it piqued my curiosity. I was naïve and curious, and I knew that if I had a bad feeling about the place I could simply turn around and walk out the door.

The photographer turned out to be a guy who used to come into Thrifty, back in the days when I worked there, and I immediately felt at ease. Still, one of the first things I asked him was whether these photographs were going to end up on the Internet. "Of course not," he said. "You'd have to sign a release."

So I posed for a few photographs, and—in some of them—I was practically nude. It felt strange and a little dirty, and when I saw Anthony later I told him about it and he wasn't at all happy with my little adventure. His response only confirmed my reservations, so I let it go. If that's the type of modeling I was destined for, then modeling wasn't for me.

A few months later, in the summer of 2000, I found out I was pregnant. I thought the father was Anthony but it later turned out that I was wrong. By the end of my first trimester, Anthony and I had gone our separate ways anyway.

I was well aware that it was going to be tough, both emotionally and financially. I quit school and took two waitressing jobs, serving food by day and cocktails by night, and started trying to save my money. It was misery being on my feet all the time. Plus I knew I'd be fired the moment I started to show.

I took long walks and talked to God. I sought His help to carry me through, to give me guidance and to provide for my needs. He had helped me in the past, but now I was having a child alone and the responsibility seemed overwhelming. I knew I couldn't make it by myself. One day I decided to give my life fully and completely to God.

The results were almost immediate. I knew that God was listening, and that knowledge alone took a huge weight off my shoulders. It was clear that I wasn't alone, and that I didn't have to struggle alone.

Before long, things started falling into place. I found a job at a machine shop for twenty-five hours a week. That type of job might sound odd to some women, but to me it was a Godsend. I could sit at my desk and do my work and I even found time to crochet a blanket for my baby. A few weeks into it, a part-time teaching position opened up at the school where I used to teach, and before long I was once again enjoying the company of children.

The next thing I knew, I found a perfect little guest house. It was warm, cozy, and affordable, and, at 800 square feet, just perfect for a young mother and her new baby.

My daughter Ayiana was born on February 20, 2001, ten days after my twenty-sixth birthday. I was still working—it was my last day of work—when I went into labor. My mother and sister and two of my close friends were there for the birth, and it was a happy occasion. I took six months off to bond with my daughter and lived very frugally on the money I'd managed to squirrel away. Then I decided to go back to school, to become a massage therapist, but I needed child care for Ayiana. I asked AFDC (Aid to Families with Dependent Children) for a little help. They came through for me and I started taking classes at Golden State, a business college with a generous financial aid program. The state paid for a portion of my education, and loaned me the money for the rest—and I've been paying that loan off regularly ever since.

My sister, Ava, wasn't working at the time, and I arranged for her to take care of Ayiana part time and to collect some of the money I was receiving from AFDC. I didn't have a dime to spare, of course, but I had faith. If I hung in there, I was confident that I would somehow find a way to provide for my daughter and myself.

My sister was incredulous. "Amber," she said one day, "how do you do it?"

I didn't know how I did it. It was hard, but I still felt blessed. I had a beautiful daughter and a cozy home, and I was getting close to getting my certification in massage therapy.

I found myself thinking back to what Aunt Nanny had told me many years earlier—"Amber, you're going to be a massage therapist some day"—and how awful it had sounded to me at the time. But on March 5, 2002, I graduated as a certified massage therapist—and was even recognized with a special award for my hard work. I had completed my academic requirement by doing 190 hours of internship, which included thirty hours with a local chiropractor. That chiropractor subsequently referred me to another chiropractor, Dave Markovich, and he hired me as a massage therapist. It was my first professional gig, and I loved it.

Ava was duly impressed with me. She was having difficulties of her own, and she was under the impression that I was sailing through life without a care in the world. This wasn't the case, of course, but I did have someone on my side. "I've given my life to God," I explained. "He is taking care of me and Ayiana."

I gave her an example: "Yesterday I was giving a client a massage, and I was absolutely broke, and I remembered that Ayiana needed diapers. And when the massage was over, my client gave me a twenty dollar tip, which was completely unexpected, and suddenly I had enough for the diapers."

Things like that were happening to me all the time. I never had anything extra, but somehow all my basic needs were being met.

My life was suddenly very full. I was working and raising my child and enjoying motherhood. I was also enjoying the business end of my life. I felt strong and independent and the future seemed full of promise. I was very happy with Ayiana and our little house in Rolling Hills, and I found a new church I really liked, the North Park Community Church.

I was lonely, of course, I admit it. It would have been nice to have a man in my life, someone to share my days and nights with, someone to come home to, but I didn't want to rush unthinkingly into my next relationship. I was being cautious, and if that meant I'd have to be lonely for a while longer, so be it. Men were complicated, and relations between men and women were doubly complicated, and the next time a man smiled at me I would think twice before smiling back.

In any event, I was focused on my career, which was really zipping along. I enjoyed working with Dave Markovich, and I was building a steady clientele, and before long I realized that I wanted to go into business for myself. I had even made inquiries about becoming an esthetician, which is in the health-care field, same as massage, but less physically demanding.

When I told Dave that I was thinking of moving on, he tried to talk me out of leaving. He said his clients liked me, and that I was good for his business. But I told him that I'd been asking around, and that I'd made inquiries at American Body Works, an establishment that would give me the autonomy I was looking for. Dave wasn't thrilled, but he understood. "I wouldn't be much of a friend if I stood in your way," he said.

I didn't make my move until mid-November, 2002. I went over to American Body Works and met with the owner for a second time, and he agreed to lease me a room in his building. I was a little nervous when I left. I had to come up with four hundred dollars within a week, and things were still very tight financially. I returned to Dave's for my last day of work, and a woman arrived for a massage—a referral. She really enjoyed the massage, and she said she wanted to see me on a regular basis. I explained that I was moving my practice to American Body Works, and that my schedule would be very flexible as soon as I made the move, and she was delighted and immediately wrote me a check for five hundred dollars. I saw the hand of God in this, too.

This was the same client who, many weeks later, would ask me how Scott Peterson's wife had died—whether it had been a long illness or a sudden death. "You need to know so you can understand what he went through," she would say.

At that time, Scott and I were still in the middle of our whirlwind romance. I was walking on air. I had only just met him, and I had no idea what lay ahead, but I knew that I was crazy about him. He was smart and funny and charming and considerate and seemed devoted to both Ayiana and me, and even if he had lied to me about being married, well—it was understandable: the poor man had suffered a terrible loss. And he had apologized for his little lie, hadn't he? He had even wept copiously when he apologized. He was still injured, still grieving, and I needed to be patient with him—needed to help him through his loss.

But of course that had been a lie, too. He hadn't lost his wife—not the way he put it, anyway. She was gone, yes, but at that point—December 30,

2002, the day I gave my interview to the police—no one really knew what had happened.

After the police were done with the interview, they invited Shawn and me to lunch. I couldn't stop thinking about Scott, or about his pregnant wife, Laci, and when we got to the restaurant I couldn't help myself: "What do you think happened to her?"

The two detectives exchanged a look. The seconds ticked by. When Al Brocchini finally spoke, I wished I hadn't asked the question. "Off the record, you want my opinion—she's dead."

My heart sank, and I guess Detective Buehler must have seen it on my face. "That's one man's opinion," he said quickly.

"That's true," Brocchini agreed. "But in my experience, a case like this—she's dead."

"But you're not sure?" I ventured.

"No."

I took a moment. "Can I do anything?"

"You're doing it," Detective Buehler said.

"No," I said. "There must be more. If there's still a chance she's alive, I want to do whatever I can to help you find her."

It was crazy. I'd never met Laci Peterson, and all I'd ever seen of her was a grainy photograph on the Internet. But I wanted to help her. I wanted to believe that she and her child were alive and that I could keep them alive and bring them home safely. It was the oddest feeling. I thought Laci Peterson needed me; I thought she was counting on me to bring her and her baby home.

"How would you feel about taping your calls?" Buehler said after a pause.

"What do you mean?" I asked.

"With Scott. What if you played along? What if you pretended you knew nothing about this, and you just acted like he was calling from Europe, and that he was still your boyfriend, and that you couldn't wait for him to come home?"

"You think that would help?" I asked.

"Absolutely," he replied. "At this point, we can't exclude Scott as a suspect. And no matter how it turns out, taping his calls would be very useful."

Buehler must have seen the concern in my eyes. "I know it's a lot to ask," he said. "And you don't have to say yes. But if you do, rest assured that we will help you in any way we can."

"That's okay," I said after a pause. "I want to help. Even if there's only a small chance she's alive, I'll do whatever it takes."

Buehler and Brocchini looked at me for a long time, and I could even feel Shawn's eyes on me.

"Where do we start?" I asked.

*"Oh my God! Laci's baby is due
on my birthday!"*

After lunch, Jon Buehler and Al Brocchini took us across the street, to a Radio Shack, and they bought a simple earpiece that I could attach to my cell phone. Unlike most earpieces, however, this one had two wires, and the second wire could be plugged into a tape recorder. Buehler gave me the microrecorder he had used to tape my interview, along with a number of empty tapes.

As we were heading back to the car, the phone rang, and I could see from the caller ID that it was Scott. I tried to start the recorder, but I was so nervous my hands were shaking, and when I finally answered the phone, the call died before I even heard Scott's voice.

"Relax," Buehler said. "He doesn't know you're taping him. Only you know and we know. It's going to take a little while to get used to, but you'll get it. Just do the best you can."

Buehler had a very generous soul. I thanked him for his patience, and for his support, and he drove us back to my place. I hurried inside with Shawn, packed a few things, and took off. Knowing what I knew about Scott, there was no way I was going to stay in my place, alone with Ayiana.

By the time we'd picked up Ayiana at school, and made it back to the Bensons', my stomach was in knots. Shawn and I told them about the police interview, and how I'd been asked to tape Scott's phone calls. Almost immediately my cell phone rang. It was Scott. I tried not to panic.

"Okay! Okay! Everybody go away! I have to do this alone. I have to focus if I'm going to get through this!" Everyone scattered, giving me a little privacy, and I let the phone ring one more time. I reminded myself that Scott was in Europe, and that I had to sound like I was convinced he was in Europe, then I started the tape and answered the phone. As I did so, I noticed that my palms were damp with sweat.

"Hello?"

"Amber? Hey—are you there? I can hardly hear you."

"I'm here."

"I can barely hear you," he repeated.

There was a lot of static on the line.

"What?" I asked.

"Hey, I'll be in . . . I'll be in Paris tomorrow. I'm flying to Normandy right now and hopefully the phone will be better. So I . . . I can't hear you right now. Are you there?"

"Can you hear me?" I asked.

"Amber?"

"Yes?"

"Okay. If you can hear me I'll be in Paris tomorrow. I'm taking a (flight) from out in the country in Normandy, so I'll call you tomorrow."

"Okay."

"I hope you hear me. I miss you. If you can hear me, bye."

"Bye."

He was nowhere near Normandy, of course. He was in the La Loma neighborhood of Modesto, and in fact had only recently been interviewed by detectives. He told them he had last seen Laci on December 24, at 9:30 a.m., when he left their home for a solo fishing trip to Berkeley, about an hour and a half away. The police subsequently searched Scott's home and his place of business, taking two computers from the house, along with Laci's Land Rover and Scott's truck.

The moment I got off the phone, I called Buehler. I was practically crying, and my hands were shaking so badly I dropped the phone. "I spoke to him," I said. "And I got it on tape."

"Great!" he said. "Did he say anything of interest?"

"No, not really. But we only talked for a few seconds."

"How are you feeling?" he asked. "You sound a little shaky."

"*Very* shaky," I said.

"Well, I'm very proud of you," he said. "You're going to be fine. Just keep doing what you're doing and try not to overthink it. And get some sleep."

The next day, the last day of the year, Scott called. "I'm uh . . . near the Eiffel Tower," he said. "The New Year's celebration is unreal. The crowd is huge . . . If you can hear me, um—it'll be nine o'clock here in the morning and I'm going to try and call you back on New Year's, *your* New Year's."

I got that on tape, too, and when he called back later, I was ready for him. I could hear barking in the background. "There is this fucking dog next to this hotel," Scott said irritably.

"This what?"

"This dog that just keeps barking."

"Really?"

"I want to kill it."

There was no hotel, of course, and the dog was his own dog—the pet he'd shared with Laci. It was beyond belief. His wife and child were missing, and he kept feeding me lies—kept making up stories out of whole cloth. How did he manage it?

I kept telling myself to act normal, and to ask the types of normal questions I would likely ask in regular conversation, and at one point I asked if he had made any New Year's resolutions. "Oh, I'm sure there's all kinds of things that I want to do better about myself," he replied, "but I've got nothing. I can't think of nothing right now off the top of my head." Then he changed the subject: he said he'd been thinking a great deal about me, and about us.

That struck me as very bizarre indeed. At that very moment, more than a thousand people were taking part in a candlelight vigil in East La Loma Park. It had been a full week since Laci had disappeared.

When I got off the phone, Paul and Lauren and everyone else were staring at me. They were understandably curious. They wanted to know what he'd said.

"He's still pretending he's in Europe," I told them. "It sounds like he's doing weird things to the phone to make it sound like there's static or something."

I called Buehler to report in. "I heard a siren in the background, and it was a regular, American siren, not like the sirens you hear in foreign movies," I said. "I can't believe Scott really thinks he's pulling this off."

"Wow," he replied. "I'm surprised you picked that up. We ought to make you a detective."

At the stroke of midnight—this was January 1, 2003—I was at Shawn's house, at a party, trying to keep my mind off Scott, when he called again. I already had the phone in my hand, knowing he would call, and I bolted down the hall and locked myself in Shawn's bathroom.

For some strange reason, I was suddenly overwhelmed by the sound of his voice, and I got very emotional: "I guess I was just so excited you know . . . to hear from you . . . I was just praying . . . oh God, please let this phone call go through and all I ask is twenty minutes, please, that's it . . . I want to hear all these things you thought about us."

It was crazy. I had taken the time to set up the recorder, and I was recording the call, and of course I knew he wasn't in Europe. But I also knew I had to be convincing, and maybe I'd made it *too* real. Ironically, there was still a small part of me that missed him, or missed the person I thought he was. Only two days earlier, despite my mounting reservations about Scott Peterson, I had still been thinking of our future together. I thought we'd get through the doubts, and that there'd be a valid explanation for everything. That at the end of the day it was me; that *I* was the problem; that there were things I hadn't fully grasped.

And clearly Scott wanted me to believe that we had a solid future. Even then, on the phone, with Laci missing and hundreds of people searching for her, he took the time to tell me that our relationship was very beautiful, and that it would evolve over time. "You know, in my mind, we could be wonderful together," he said. "I could care for you in any and every way."

I again called Buehler, as I did every time I connected with Scott. I was generally able to hold it together when I had Scott on the line, but the moment I heard Buehler's voice I would feel myself coming unglued—my hands and voice would shake, I had to take deep breaths to steady myself—but he always managed to calm me down. He said he had great confidence in me, and he was never less than 110 percent supportive.

The following morning, as I began to do every morning, and sometimes even three or four times a day, I logged onto the Laci Peterson website. I discovered that thousands of people were praying for her, and sending words of love and encouragement to the family, and I was heartened by the photographs of her—a lovely, pregnant mother-to-be, smiling radiantly and glowing with optimism and good health.

Later in the day, I was flipping through issues of *The Modesto Bee*, the local newspaper, when I saw something I took for a sign. *Oh my God*, I thought, bursting into tears. *Laci's baby is due on my birthday!*

I called Buehler, freaking out, and he tried to calm me down. For a moment, I had a horrible feeling that I'd misdialed, and that I was actually talking to Scott. I believed he knew I'd gone to the police, and that that was him on the phone, messing with my head.

"Scott?"

"Amber, it's me. Buehler. I'm right here. I'm not going anywhere. Talk to me."

I thought I was losing my mind, and Buehler was understandably concerned. "You know what, Amber? You've done enough; more than enough. I'm worried about you. Maybe we should stop this now."

"But we haven't found Laci," I said, snapping out of it and pulling myself together. "I want to keep trying."

"You amaze me," Buehler said. "I don't know too many women who could handle this. I'm grateful for your strength."

"It's not me," I said. "It's God—God is giving me the strength."

When I got off the phone, I remember gazing out the window and thinking that God had been preparing me for this. Young as I was, I'd had more than my share of drama and heartache, and it had made me a stronger person. And, strange as it sounds, I was thankful. I didn't know why God had chosen me for this ordeal, but I was somehow suited to it and knew that I would see it through to the end. I would do whatever I could to help. My most ardent hope was that these conversations would lead to Laci, and that we would find her and her child alive.

I could do this. I *knew* I could do it. After all, God doesn't give us more than we can handle. First Corinthians 10:13: "No temptation has seized you except what is common to man. And God is faithful. He will not let you be tempted beyond what you can bear. But when you are tempted, He will also provide a way out so that you can stand up under it." Scott called again at around ten o'clock that night. He told me that he had arrived in Brussels from Paris and that he was about to go for a morning jog. He said he was gaining weight from all the rich French food, and described himself as "pudge boy." He talked about jogging down to the main square, "with all the big churches in the background," and about "tripping on cobblestones."

"So how much do you weigh now?" I said, trying to keep it light.

"I don't know. I don't have a scale . . . You sound chipper."

"Oh," I said, "I always am when I hear from you."

"Chipper's kind of a bad word," he observed.

"Chipper?"

"Not a bad word," he said, correcting himself, "but kind of a gay word."

After we got off the phone, my head was spinning. I thought, *This guy is unbelievable. His wife is missing and presumed dead, and he's talking about French food and big churches and cobblestones.*

The following day, he called again. He asked me to watch the Warren Beatty remake of *Love Affair*, and said that Beatty was one of his heroes. He told me that the mere memory of the film brought tears to his eyes, and added: "Love doesn't mean that people can be together forever."

I didn't know what he was trying to tell me— Was he talking about Laci? Was he talking about us?—and I didn't have the wherewithal to question him.

Later in that same conversation, he said: "I have a picture of you guys here." He meant me and Ayiana. The picture had been taken over Thanksgiving, at Shawn's house. "I've been carrying it in my suit pocket," he added.

On January 2, I learned from news reports that police were asking the public for help in verifying Scott's alibi. They said he had receipts related to his fishing trip, but no one actually remembered seeing him—either at the marina or on the river—and they were hoping someone might step forward with information. They released photographs of Scott's boat and truck, hoping this would help.

When I thought about this, it seemed unreal.

The Laci Peterson disappearance had become a huge, national story. Reporters were enthralled. They all focused on the same thing: a young, successful couple who seemed to have everything, with a child on the way, and now the wife was missing under increasingly mysterious circumstances. None of them described Scott as a suspect, of course, not yet, anyway. But they didn't have to: everyone seemed to think he was behind it.

I know Scott was nervous about all the press coverage. In our conversations, he would make references to things he'd seen in the local paper—the migration of the monarch butterflies, say, or a bombing overseas—to see if I was following the news. I *was* following the news, of course. I read the papers, watched television, and surfed the Web. But I wasn't about to let him know it. There was something else I wasn't going to let him know, which is that it sickened me to see Laci's family on the news, still being supportive of Scott. I knew the truth about him— that he was a world-class liar—but they didn't know it. And I wasn't at liberty to tell them.

On the morning of January 3, I told myself I was going to pay less attention to the case—that I would try to get on with my life. Preschool was about to get under way, I had my job at American Body Works, and I longed for normalcy. I'd also been invited to a party that night, the pajama version of a Tupperware party, and at the very least I thought it would help take my mind off this ongoing telephone drama with Scott.

Ayiana had been at my sister's for two nights, and we had arranged to meet at Dad's place later, where I would pick her up. At this point, Ava was divorced, with two kids of her own, and she had recently moved in with someone I didn't know very well. I didn't think there was anything to worry about, but as a mother you want to know where your child is, and who he or she is spending time with. Ironically, Ava's new home was in Modesto, not far from Scott's neighborhood.

When I went over to my dad's, looking for Ayiana, no one was there. I ran all over town looking for her, in a panic, and finally found her at mom's house. I was hugely relieved—but I was also worn down with exhaustion and worry, and feeling very much at the end of my rope. The minute Ava walked into the room, I noticed that her bare feet were covered in mud, and I just snapped. "How could you?!" I shouted.

I knew right away that she had been out searching for Laci, as so many locals were doing at the time, and I didn't think my family needed to become any more involved than it already was.

"Me?!" she snapped back. "This is all your fault. If you weren't out dating every loser in the book, our family wouldn't be going through this."

That really hurt, and I just lost it. Before I knew it, there were fuck yous back and forth, and I grabbed Ayiana and got out of there. I was shaking with rage, but I pulled myself together for my daughter.

When Scott called later that day, I was a complete mess. I felt so alone that I started sobbing. I told him that I'd had a fight with Ava, and that it had turned ugly, but I didn't go into a lot of detail. Before I knew it, he was comforting me, and for a moment I forgot that I was talking to the Scott Peterson who was about to become the prime suspect in his wife's disappearance.

"Can I tell you how wonderful you are?" he said. "That's pretty easy to do. How thoughtful you are and amazing . . . It's an amazing combination of attributes that you have. . . . And I need a bigger better word than 'special' to describe it. . . . That's what I was thinking about today. I need a better vocabulary or a book or a thesaurus or something to find the right words to describe you."

He went on at length, and he was very convincing: "If you cross the words eclectic and special and thoughtful and caring . . . (you get) the word used in the Bible for love: Agape."

But apparently he still didn't think he was do-

ing me justice. "(I)t's like I'm drawing a stick figure," he said. "I'm that far removed from being
able to describe you."

After the call ended, I began to wonder what
words one might use to describe Scott Peterson.
Pathological liar, no doubt. I also remembered
seeing that someone on the Internet called him a
sociopath. I didn't know whether Scott had had
anything to do with Laci's disappearance, of
course, but if he had, the word fit him to a tee.
According to a definition I found on the Internet,
sociopaths are charming and manipulative and
lie with impunity. They feel no shame or remorse. They are incapable of love. They are de-
void of empathy. And they are parasitic. One of
the articles said they make "all-encompassing
promises for the future." Was that Scott? Isn't
that what he'd been doing? It was very debilitat-
ing. I had been looking for someone to love, and
I had ended up with this.

I was tired of having my heart broken. Every
relationship with a man started out so full of
promise, and they all ended so badly. I had to
figure out what I was doing wrong.

That same day, I came across a story in which
a friend of Scott's described a recent evening at
the Petersons'. He said Scott had spilled red
wine on the couch, and that Laci became very
upset. This would have seemed like an insignifi-

cant detail to most people, but it struck home with me. Scott had once spilled wine on *my* couch, and I had just laughed it off. I was mystified by the look of gratitude that had come over his face. "You are so great," he had said effusively. "I can't believe you didn't throw a fit over that, like most women."

"You don't have to thank me," I'd said.

"I do," he had said. "Thank you for just being you." It was impossible not to think about him, and it was driving me crazy. I called Dave Markovich and went over to his place. I needed someone to talk to. I asked him if he'd heard about Laci Peterson, and he said it rang a very faint bell, so I explained who she was and explained my involvement in the case. "Well, that guy—her husband—Scott Peterson," I stammered. "That was the guy I was dating."

Dave was a little stunned, to say the least. I told him the whole sordid story, and he listened patiently.

"I can't believe it," he said.

"I know. Neither can I."

He took a moment. "Well, you know—whatever happens, I'm here for you."

"Thank you," I said. "You have no idea how much that means to me. You have no idea how frightened and alone I feel."

* * *

The following day, January 4, Scott was still pretending to be in Europe, and still faking poor reception. At one point, he said: "Ooh! The best movie ever made is *The Shining*. . . . It scares the hell out of me." I was instantly struck by his choice: As I remembered it, Jack Nicholson plays a character who tries to kill his wife and young son.

I tried to get Scott to change the subject. It was late, and I didn't want to go to bed thinking about that movie. I had enough to deal with. Being on the phone with Scott was exhausting and unnerving, and—with the exception of Detective Buehler, who was effusive with his praise—I had to handle him pretty much on my own. And it was a real balancing act: I knew he wasn't in Paris, and I knew he was lying, but I couldn't let him know I knew. I had to keep him on the line, and I had to fight the urge to scream at him, and to call him on his lies.

It was hard even when I wasn't on the phone with him. If I was expecting one of his calls, I would psyche myself up like an athlete before a game. I would pace back and forth, and keep reminding myself, out loud, that Scott was calling from Paris or Brussels or Normandy. I would repeat this to myself over and over, and it became a sort of ritual. I remember doing this over at the Bensons', who began to wonder if I was losing my mind.

"Amber, you do know he's not in Paris, right?"

Yes. I knew. But that didn't make it any easier. Especially for an honest person. I can't believe how hard I found it to tell lies.

Scott went from horror films to romance. He quoted from "Hops," a Boris Pasternak poem. It begins as follows:

> *Beneath the willow wound round with ivy*
> *we take cover from the worst*
> *of the storm, with a greatcoat round*
> *our shoulders and my hands around your waist.*

"I just like that first stanza because it sounded so much like, you know, two people providing shelter for each other," he said. "We huddle under a large tree wound with ivy with the storm raging around us. The only thing keeping me grounded are my hands on your waist."

He didn't sound grounded at all.

"Do you think I'm intelligent?" I asked him, trying to steer him in another direction.

"Yeah, but that wasn't the quality I was thinking of."

"Tell me?" I asked.

"Self-esteem. You have good self-esteem, and that's difficult to find in people."

"So you've been thinking a lot about me?" I prodded.

"Yeah, that's all I did today," he said, his voice

breaking suddenly. "And I'm sorry, I just, I just, I just started rambling and there's a tear in my eye and it's trickling."

I wondered if he was thinking about Laci and his unborn child. Were the trickling tears for them, or were they for him? I certainly didn't think they were for me. I wasn't even sure they were real.

"You know how much I need you, right?" Scott said.

"Yes," I said, playing along. I felt like crying. For real.

"You know, and I'm not just saying it."

"What was that?"

"I'm not just saying stuff."

"Well, I'd like to—"

"And you need to know how true that is and how wonderful you are. I want you to know that."

Then he talked about Jack Kerouac, a writer I wasn't familiar with, and noted that he had "never had a prolonged period of freedom like that from responsibility. . . ."

I found this chilling. Was this notion of freedom from responsibility somehow connected to Laci's disappearance?

"I'm not half the turd as I was when I was eighteen," Scott said. "(But) I'm still a turd."

I kept playing along, and sometimes I lost myself in these conversations. There were times when I almost felt sympathy for him; when he read me the Pasternak poem, for example. But when he talked about taking me on vacations and about love at first sight and about his favorite movies, I felt anger welling up inside me. I couldn't betray my feelings, though. I had come to believe, right or wrong, that we were going to find Laci, and that she was still alive. And even in those moments when I thought I might be deluding myself, I still wanted to believe that she was okay.

"Amber, I can't hear you, sweetie."

"I can hear you just fine."

A moment later, the line went dead: he kept pretending to have trouble with the international connection. It had become second nature to him.

I was back at the Bensons' again. Paul asked me how I was doing. He was very kind, very attentive. "It's hard, but I'm hanging in," I said. "I can't believe this guy. He talks to me about love, and that he can't find the words to describe me, and meanwhile Laci's nowhere to be found."

Paul did his best to comfort me. He told me I was doing great and that he was incredibly impressed with my strength, and he gave me a big hug. Paul was the uncle I never had.

On January 5, my friend Saki called and left a cryptic message on my answering machine. "Hi Amber, this is Saki. . . . Um, I'm still delayed on my trip. I got stuck in L.A. I'm in L.A. right now. Um . . . I really . . . oh, God, I really hope you're okay, Amber. Um, I'm sitting here reading *People* magazine and um . . . there's something in it that's just at this moment it just shocks me and if I don't talk to you before I get on the plane um . . . I will call you as soon as I get—I get in."

There had been an article in *People* about Laci Peterson. It had included a photograph of Scott. Saki sounded upset. I didn't realize at the time that she had sold that very photograph to *People*. I thought she was calling because she was worried about me; now I think she was probably calling because she was feeling bad about what she did.

The next day, Buehler phoned and asked if I could come to Modesto. He gave me directions to the Orchard Motel, in nearby Turlock, and I drove there and met him and Sharon Hagan, a profiler with the Department of Justice, as well as Detective Craig Grogan, of the Modesto Police Department. They had checked me in under the name *Teresa Collins*. I guess they were just being careful.

"One of the reasons I asked you to come up is because Scott is in Fresno," Buehler said. "I didn't want you to run into him. The other reason is that we want to try to help you in your next conversation with Scott."

"Help me how?" I asked.

"You're going to keep him on the phone, and we'll feed you questions from time to time. Officer Hagan is going to try to help you get some information out of him."

"I'll do what I can," I said.

It turned out to be a watershed day. It was the day Scott Peterson finally told me about Laci.

V

....

"*Isn't that a little twisted, Scott?*"

On January 6, when Scott finally called, I was sitting in a small room in the Modesto police station with Buehler and Sharon Hagan, the profiler. Detective Grogan hovered in the background.

I fumbled with the recorder, and I heard Scott say he had something to tell me, "the worst thing in the world."

"Okay," I said. I didn't know what he was going to say, but he sounded deeply affected, maybe even genuinely so, and I braced myself for it.

"And I am so sorry that this has happened," he went on. "And I'm so sorry I'm going to hurt you in this way. I don't want to do this over the phone. I want to tell you this. I want to be there in person to tell you this. But I'm sure that's why Saki called you."

"What?"

"I'm sure that's why Saki called you."

"Why? Why would Saki—what are you talking about?"

I didn't quite understand what he meant.

Then I remembered that cryptic message that Saki had left on my answering machine, which I had told Scott about.

"It's the worst thing. I'm sorry, Amber. Um, well, I'll just—I'll just tell you."

"Okay."

"Uh, you haven't been watching the news obviously . . ."

"No."

"Um, I have not been traveling for the last couple of weeks. I—I have lied to you that I've been traveling."

"Okay," I said, urging him on.

"The girl I'm married to," Scott said, "her name is Laci. She disappeared just before Christmas. For the past two weeks I've been in Modesto with her family and mine and searching for her. . . ."

"You've been calling . . . having conversations with me when all this is happening?" I replied. I tried to sound incredulous.

"Yeah."

"Really? Isn't that a little twisted, Scott?"

"It is."

"Well, at least you agree with me there."

"Well, that's the truth, isn't it?"

"You have a missing pregnant wife, and you're talking to your girlfriend? Huh! Huh! Did you think about that one?"

"It sounds terrible. . . ."

None of the police officers could hear Scott's end of the conversation, but they could hear me, and they kept scribbling little notes and setting them in front of me, urging me to ask Scott things that had never occurred to me:

"Did you have a gun?"

"Did you shoot her?"

"Where's her body?"

"Is she missing because you fell in love with me, Scott?"

I couldn't bring myself to ask everything they suggested, but I had plenty to say on my own—and the pain and anger were real. They got caught up in it, too. From time to time I'd look up to find the three of them egging me on wordlessly, cheering with upraised fists and making other gestures of support. It was surreal.

I have decided to quote from that January 6 conversation at length. It was an important day, a day of confession; it was the single, most revealing conversation I ever had with Scott Peterson. And it was pretty harrowing. But there was worse to come. Much worse.

S: For the past two weeks, I've been in Modesto, with her family and mine . . . searching for her.

A: Okay.

S: She just disappeared, and no one knows—

A: Okay, now . . .

S: —where she's been.

A: Scott?

S: And I . . . I can't tell you more because I . . . I need you to be protected from the media . . . and Ayiana.

A: Okay.

S: Okay, they are amazing.

A: Scott—.

S: Yeah.

A: —are you listening?

S: I am.

A: You came to me earlier in December and told me that you had lost your wife. What was that about?

S: She's (unintelligible) . . . she's alive.

A: What?

S: She's alive.

A: Where? She's alive? Where?

S: In Modesto. Now, I know I . . . I've . . . this is the hardest . . . I . . . I wanted to tell you in person. I . . . here . . . you need to protect yourself from the media.

A: Okay.

S: Okay. If you even watch the news at all . . . Well, you haven't. Um . . . the media . . . has been telling everyone that I had something to do with her disappearance. So the past two weeks I've been . . . hunted by the media. And I just . . . I don't want you to be involved . . . in this, to protect yourself. I know that I've, you know, I've destroyed. And I, God, I hope . . . I hope so much that . . . this doesn't hurt you.

A: How could it not affect me?

S: It does. And I just—

A: How . . . how . . . could you possibly think this would not affect me?

S: Amber, I know it does.

A: (sigh)

S: But I . . . I . . . I know I had . . . I . . . I have just been torn up the last two weeks wanting to . . . tell you and I'm so weak that I haven't. And I just . . . I just hope that . . . uh . . . I had . . . to call you and tell you that.

A: You never . . . you never answered my question, Scott?

S: Sweetie, you don't . . . you don't . . . I can't . . . I can't say anymore . . .

A: I think I deserve . . .

S: You deserve so much better. There's no question you deserve so much better.

A: Yeah, and I deserve to understand an explanation of why you told me you lost your wife and this was the first holidays you'd spend without her? That was December 9th . . . You told me this, and . . . now all of a sudden your wife's missing? . . . Are you kidding me?

S: Yeah she—

A: Did you hear me?

S: I did . . . I . . . I . . . I . . . I don't know what to say . . . I . . .

A: I think an explanation would uh . . . be a start.

S: I know you absolutely deserve an explanation, sweetie . . .

A: Yes, I do. I do.

S: And I want to give you one.

A: I'm listening.

S: I . . . I can't now . . . I mean you don't understand.

A: But I . . . I . . . I don't understand why . . .

S: You don't understand the situation . . . and . . .

A: Then why don't you fill me in on the situation, and . . . and make me understand?

S: I can't now. I'm so sorry for that.

A: Why can't you? Why?

S: It's . . . it's to protect all of us.

A: To protect all of who?

S: Everyone involved.

A: So where is she?

S: That's what . . . we are trying to find out. We have . . . it's a nationwide search. We have . . . I mean it's a half a million dollar reward for information leading to her safe return.

A: Okay. So, again, you never answered my question: Why did you tell me it would be the first holidays without her?

S: I can't. Sweetie, I can't explain anymore now.

A: When can—

S: I'm so sorry. You should be so angry at me, and God, I hope you are. I just—

A: Yeah, isn't that what you told me before, oh, I wish, you know it'd be so much easier if you'd hate me and not want to talk to me. And, and of course the . . . the person I am, of course I'm going to say well, you know, you told me you lost your wife. You sat there in front of me and cried and broke down. I sat there and held your hand, Scott, and comforted you, and you were lying to me . . .

S: Yeah.

A: —again: lying to me about lying.

S: I lied to you about traveling, yeah.

A: That's . . . among everything else. That's just an added.

S: Yeah.

A: So, again, are you going . . . is it that you're not going to answer me?

S: I want to.

A: And what's stopping you?

S: I do.

A: And what's stopping you from answering . . .

S: (unintelligible) things . . .

A: —why? Why would you tell me this on March 9th . . . ? That you have lost your wife and I'm sorry I can't tell until after I get back from Europe and about this tragedy, and I asked you are you ready for me? Oh, absolutely. This will be the first holidays without my wife. I'm going spend them with my family in Maine. Is this not what you said?

S: It is.

A: It is?

S: —and I . . . It is and I . . . it is.

138

A: And how do you explain all of a sudden you tell me it's a national search?

S: It is, yes.

A: How is that just not such a coincidence?

S: If you think I had something to do with her disappearance . . . er, it, that is so wrong.

A: Really?

S: Yes, it is.

A: And how is there such a coincidence to that story from what you're telling me about what . . . ?

S: Well, no, sweetie. I—

A: And you still have the audacity to call me "sweetie" right now? . . . First, let's see, first . . .

S: Amber?

A: —my friend lies to me about his wife, and I cried to you and tell you about this.

S: I know, I know it. I'm—

A: And then you have the audacity to say how do you handle something like this. Are you kidding me? And to put me in a position . . . And you want to protect me from the media. Why did you involve me in this? What—

S: I . . . I haven't . . .

A: —role did I play? How long were you look-ing for me, Scott?

S: I'm sorry?

A: How long were you looking for me?

S: Looking for you?

A: Yes.

S: I don't understand, Amber.

A: Weren't you looking for me? Isn't that what you told Shawn—you were looking for me . . . or someone like me? How is—

S: I want to—

A: —what . . . I . . . I . . . I am just such at a loss right now.

S: I know.

A: You say you can't tell me, you want to tell me in person. At what point are you going to tell me in person, Scott?

S: Once we find her.

A: What was that?

S: Once we find her.

A: Once we find her what?

S: And that will be, I mean—resolution. And I will be . . . I will be able to explain every-thing to you.

A: When you find her?

S: I know you can't trust me, I know you can't trust me.

A: Uh-huh.

S: I could never ask you to do that.

A: Okay, so how—

S: I could never ask you, but I . . . I just . . . I had to tell you.

A: But didn't you . . . didn't you say, "Amber, I will do anything for you to trust me. Uh . . . baby, we have . . . I feel we have a future together." What . . . what was that about?

S: I never said anything to you I didn't mean.

A: You never told me anything you didn't mean?

S: I lied to you about . . . things, I did.

A: Uh-huh. So, uh . . . how am I going to stay out of this? How . . . and . . . and uh . . . how do you see that happening? How do you see that I'm going to stay out of this or I'm not going to be dragged in or involved into this? How is that, Scott, can you answer me that?

S: I don't know, but you . . . I don't know, but you deserve to be—

A: No, I don't deserve to be . . . You're right . . .

S: —exactly—

A: —I don't—

S: —exactly, you do not deserve to be.

A: So why did you drag—

S: You don't deserve . . . the things that I've done to you, but . . . there's no but. I'm sorry, hey, I agree with you. I want to explain everything to you—

A: Yes . . .

S: —but I can't.

A: Why?

S: Um . . . primarily . . . well, there are lots of reasons. Primarily, protection, for everyone.

A: Protection of who?

S: Everyone.

A: Who is everyone?

S: Everyone is . . . is you, me, our families.

A: Everyone that would possibly look at you a little bit differently because who the hell am I? I . . . I . . . you know, you're telling me that we're . . . oh, I asked is there anybody else? "Oh, no, I'm monogamous as far as I am concerned."

S: I never cheated on you.

A: Ha, ha, ha!

S: I never did.

A: You're *married*. How do you figure you never cheated on me? Explain that one to me?

S: I want to explain, Amber.

A: And . . . you want to doesn't that mean you're going to, right? Is that—

S: I will. No, no, I will.

A: When?

S: I hope . . . I, God, I hope to hell that you will listen to me and that I can. I want to explain it to you so badly, but I can't, now. And I . . . I hope and I can never ask you to . . . to trust me or to even listen to me again.

A: There's no way . . . there's no way I possibly can.

S: I know it. I can never ask you to do that for me. And I . . . I hope that sometime in the future, you will let me tell you the whole story. And I cannot ask you . . .

A: You know what, that . . . that makes a lot more sense to me now, Scott.

S: What's that?

A: Of course you couldn't tell me the story about your wife because it hadn't happened yet. And you were hoping to resolve, in January, that it would be resolved and you'd have a story to tell me.

S: Sweetie, you think I had something to do with her disappearance? Amber, do you believe that?

A: Well, let's see how can I believe that? How can I believe that? How could I believe anything for—

S: I am not . . . evil like that.

A: I would hope not.

S: I am . . . Oh my God!

A: You know you've lied to me now . . . and, you know . . . you know, uh . . . actually, you know, I was thinking, um . . . do you know how many people I've given your picture to . . . or of us, in Christmas cards? So you're telling me . . . that you want to keep me out of this and Ayiana, and you want to protect me from that. How? I'm . . . I'm just . . . I'm just so at a loss. I . . . how . . .

S: Amber, I . . . I had to tell you. I've been wanting to tell you. I hope in the future, I can tell you everything . . . if you'll let me. I can never ask you to trust me and I am so sorry that . . . I have . . . I've—that this has happened and this is happening to you. And that is, uh . . . just the truth. And . . .

A: You know when I met you . . .

S: It hurts—

A: It hurts me.

S: —it hurts me you believe that I could have something to do with her disappearance.

A: But, you know—

S: But I understand your anger.

A: You know what, actually . . . I . . . I've never . . . I have not said that, those words have not come out of my mouth, Scott, now have they?

S: Everyone has been pointing a finger at me and I just—

A: No, those came out of your mouth. And I'm not one to judge. There's only one.

S: I know you aren't. But yeah, that's very true.

A: But isn't that ironic how, Scott, when I first met you on our date, how you told me you were going to Maine with your family and you were going to Paris and Europe and all these things? And then you came to me after Shawn had found out that you were married and you came and told me this elaborate lie about her missing and this tragedy and that . . .

S: No.

A: And that . . . that this will be the first holidays without her?

S: Sweetie, I never said . . . Amber, I . . .

A: Yes?

S: I . . . God, I don't want to fight with you. Um . . . you know that I . . . I never said tragedy or missing.

A: Oh, yes, you said you've lost your wife.

S: No . . . That—that, yes.

A: You said obviously without me saying much, but we were . . .

S: I said that I lost my wife.

A: Yes, you did.

S: I did. And yes—

A: How did you lose her then, before she was lost? Explain that?

S: There's different kinds of loss, Amber.

A: Then explain your loss?

S: I . . . I can't to you now.

A: When can you?

S: I can once there's—

A: When my name has been smeared all over the tabloids and everything else because I'm the . . . the . . . the "lover." I'm the "girlfriend" . . . When you've had, when you've been married to this woman?

S: You don't deserve that.

A: No, I don't deserve this. And you say you've been faithful to me. Oh, I've—"some people I tell I've been married and other people I say I never have because it's so painful for me."

S: I've lied to you.

A: Oh, more than—many times, apparently. You know . . . when you sat me down . . . remember I said, "Oh, I thought you were gonna tell me you were married?"

S: Right.

A: So—so Scott, what about your baby? Laci's . . . missing woman, pregnant, is that what you said?

S: Yes.

A: Really? So is that why—

S: I want . . . I want . . .

A: Yes?

S: I want to explain all of this to you now.

A: Yes? I'm listening.

S: And I . . . I just am not able to.

A: Why?

S: I can't ask you to trust me, but you will . . . If you give me a chance later to explain it.

A: Later when? I'm listening right now.

S: You will thank me for . . . what's that?

A: I will thank you for what?

S: You will thank me for not explaining it now.

A: Really?

S: Not thank me, but you'll understand. And I can't ask you to even listen to me . . . I can't do that.

A: Well, I—

S: And this is the hardest thing . . . You can't even believe that, I understand.

A: Yeah. Is that why you said you didn't want to have any children and Ayiana was the only child you ever see of having and . . . and at that point assuming we're together she would be . . . you would have her as your own? Why would you tell me when you were expecting a baby?

S: Sweetie, I . . . I'm so sorry I can't tell you everything now.

A: Why can't you tell me everything? *Why*?

S: There is simply . . . It just has entirely too many repercussions and they're not all for me.

148

A: —and you're what?

S: Okay . . . There's a lot and all the repercussions don't deal with me.

A: What repercussions? What repercussions?

S: If I was to explain, explain to you—

A: Yes?

S: —and you, you know the media started attacking you . . . or anything else, so many people would be hurt.

A: (sigh)

S: But I mean I—I can understand that you could never believe what I am saying, I pray to God I just, I hope you do, but I . . . I can understand . . . I'm so sorry . . .

A: Tell me the coincidence of Laci, your wife, disappearing and your stories earlier in December? And then you . . . you're carrying on this elaborate lie with me that you're in Europe . . . and you're in Maine with your folks? Explain that to me?

S: I wanted to tell you about this—

A: Really?

S: —as . . . as soon as it happened.

A: But of course you couldn't because you were in Maine with your folks, huh?

S: No, I didn't make that trip.

A: So, you know, you and I—

S: —are destroyed . . .

A: You and I, assuming we'd be together, how would you have explained the baby, that you . . . brought into this world?

S: I'm sorry . . .

A: How would you explain your baby to me?

S: Sweetie, you don't know everything.

A: No, I didn't, so what . . . what is it?

S: I want to tell you everything, but I can't.

A: Okay, are you listening to me?

S: I am.

A: Okay, how . . . now again, you were assuming we would stay together and you tell me about all these future things with me. How would you explain a newborn child of yours, that I mean I would assume she would want you to have regular visits with this child . . . right?

S: Sweetie, I'm so sorry but I can't tell you—

A: Why can't you?

S: —about those things right now.

A: Why? Why? Why not right now?

S: It would hurt entirely too many people.

A: Now is this child yours?

S: Sweetie . . . I'm sorry I keep saying that, you asked me not to. Amber, I cannot tell you.

A: Is this child yours?

S: I can't tell you all these things right now.

A: Why?

S: The only . . . the only things I just I needed you to know and I hope that . . . I hope that . . . you are not . . . you know . . . God, I . . . I . . . I think I know I hurt you.

A: You hope what?

S: Amber?

A: Yes.

S: Amber?

A: You hope what?

S: I just hope that I mean you don't get more hurt by this than I'm doing.

A: You don't know what I've gone through and for you to have no compassion for me.

S: I hope you don't think that's true.

A: You know actions speak louder than words.

S: That's true.

A: That's one for you to ponder for a while.

S: It's true. I deserve everything you say. There's no question, Amber.

A: So tell me, Scott.

S: Yeah?

A: Why should I not go to the police with this?

S: It's your decision.

A: Really?

S: Of course.

A: And at that point, uh . . . I go to the police, um . . . I don't know. I don't know if they would, uh, release it to the media or, you know, obviously they would question you, they would want to know everything.

S: Uh . . . I don't know . . . I mean it's your decision, of course. Uh . . . I . . . I wanted to tell you . . . what has happened, and I wanted to tell you that I lied to you.

A: And what stopped you from . . . from this?

S: Previous to now?

A: Yeah.

S: You know I could make excuses how to justify it to myself . . . about—

A: You're not doing too great right now.

S: Well, I know—I'm trying. I justify it to myself by saying no, she just found out about . . . , no, she just had a fight with her sister, don't tell her. No, no, it was probably just weakness and hoping that I could hold onto you.

A: Just a weakness and . . . and holding onto me?

S: Longing to hold onto you.

A: Longing to hold onto me?

S: And not being able to tell you about me traveling, Amber?

A: Yes.

S: Are you there?

A: Yeah, I'm here.

S: I deserve everything you want to say to me.

A: Well, again, you know Shawn said . . .

S: I'm sorry . . . Amber?

A: Are you forgetting things you had discussed with Shawn? "If you're not serious about a relationship, don't call Amber. She's been through too much already." Do you remember having this discussion with Shawn?

S: Yeah, I remember.

A: Oh! But you went ahead and went through. Why? Why? Are you there? Hello?

S: Amber?

A: Yes.

S: Amber?

A: Do you hear me? Are you driving? Hello? If you can't hear me call me back.

Before he called back, the profiler pointed out that he was still lying—that it seemed to be pathological with him. "He lies even when he doesn't have to lie. He's lying about little things. Every time he says the phrase 'My God,' he's lying. He's even lying about lying." Then the phone rang. It was Scott again.

For some strange reason, I wanted to hear him say he was innocent, and I asked him outright if he was in any way connected to this mystery.

"My God, Amber, I had nothing to do with her disappearance," he said.

"Then who did?"

"We don't have any idea."

"Really?"

"There was a robbery here and, you know, there's—

"You think a robber had something to do with her disappearance?"

"—across from the house where she disappeared there was a robbery that morning."

"Uh-huh. And?"

"Well, obviously—"

"Well, robbers don't steal people, *pregnant* people, for that."

I looked up at Detective Buehler. He was beaming. "Atta girl!" he whispered.

Then I went back to the phone: "I'm telling you," he said, "the police—those are the leads they've indicated."

"Oh, those are the only leads they've indicated?"

"Yeah . . ."

And later still, exhausted: "You can't tell me honestly you think she's been abducted for her baby?" I asked.

And Scott replied: "That's the only thought I could have."

I asked him why he had kept talking to me throughout the ordeal, and he said that it cheered him up, and that he had been trying "to gain courage to tell you about the situation."

And when I again pressed him for details, he said, "Well, I mean we're running in circles about the things we can't talk about." To which I replied, "We're running around in circles? Okay, then, why don't you lead me down a straight path into understanding?"

He kept insisting he couldn't talk, and I kept pushing him: "Are you psychic? I mean, you predicted your wife would be missing. . . . This is the biggest coincidence ever."

No, he protested. He said he wasn't "evil like that," and he began to cry.

"Save your tears," I snapped. "I did everything possible to protect my baby and me. I told you this. I worked forty-plus hours a week—because I wasn't going to ask for any help from anyone. And I did this on my own. I went to school. I had my baby, I did this all with her. I didn't need this in my life. I didn't need for someone to come in and to fuck all of it up."

I was starting to lose it. No more clever questions. This was raw emotion.

"I know that, Amber," he said, crying openly now.

"You weren't supposed to be someone that would bring me down!"

"No, I don't want to be."

"You were supposed to be someone to be there for me."

When it was over, when I was sitting there, spent, drying my tears, Sharon Hagan asked if I wanted counseling.

"I'm okay," I said. "I'll talk to my pastor."

I probably did need counseling. I looked at Buehler. "You did great," he said.

"Did I?"

"Yes," he answered me, and I could see he meant it.

I was relieved, but at the same time I felt indescribably sad.

Scott hadn't told me anything that was going to help them find Laci, and when I looked at their faces I remembered what Detective Al Brocchini had said not all that long ago: "Off the record, you want my opinion—she's dead."

I kept thinking that none of this was really

happening. That I'd been in a terrible accident, or that I was asleep, and that at any moment I would wake up.

But I didn't wake up.

VI

....

*"I know I'm innocent.
They know I'm innocent.
Everyone close to this knows I'm innocent."*

On January 7, I went back to the Modesto Police Department to try again. It wasn't long before my cell phone rang.

That second day was every bit as intense as the first. I lied to Scott, telling him I was at my mom's house, using her computer. I told him I was researching the case online, trying to make sense of things. And I accused him of not doing all he could to bring Laci back.

"You have nothing to hide?" I asked him at one point.

"No."

"And so you're fine?"

"Yes."

"And so then wouldn't I read somewhere that you're . . . that . . . that . . . that there's no possible way you're a suspect? At this point they haven't ruled that out, Scott."

"Yeah, well, as you read it and as you know this case is going, unfortunately there is . . . everyone is a suspect . . . I'm (a) prime suspect, um, you know, and all they say is they haven't ruled me out, but they haven't ruled me in."

It was odd. Here he was talking about the police, and about being a prime suspect in the case, thinking that I was at my mom's house, when all along I was sitting in a room with the very men and women who were intent on catching him.

Later in our conversation, he said, "I did a *Good Morning America* spot.'"

"You did a *Good Morning America* spot?"

"Yeah, the day after Christmas. And I made the producer promise me that they would show her photo and the number and the reward."

"Uh-huh."

"And I made her promise me that four times, and they didn't."

"Really?"

"All they showed was me. So I've learned quickly that the media will not do that unless that's all they have."

"Uh-huh."

"And we have a media consultant here, and it's her theory that this is how it should be done also."

And later still:

". . . it's brutal to hear that I'm guilty. I walk up to people on the street when I'm out, you know, knocking door to door, and people tell me without knowing who I am that I had something to do with this. . . ."

"Scott, you know, I'm concerned . . . I'm concerned and I'm looking . . . I'm looking past this right now that even if we continued in a relationship we could be out for dinner one night and the cops could come over . . . or at our home or whatever . . . and arrest you for Laci's murder. . . ." I didn't believe I'd ever be out to dinner with him again, but I wanted to do everything I could to help the police, and if that little white lie helped, I could live with it. "How can I be sure this . . . this will not occur?"

"Because I had nothing to do with it. You know, the only indication in that realm that I'll have is when they find her."

"So how are you going to plea your innocence?"

"I don't have to. I know I'm innocent. They know I'm innocent. Everyone close to this knows I'm innocent. I don't care about the media or the, you know, 70 percent of the population out there who's ignorant and foolish and, you know, immediately jumps to conclusions . . ."

At one point, Scott tried to woo me with religion. "I've got my Bible in front of me," he said, and he referred to the Parable of the Sower:

"Luke 8:4–8: And when much people were gathered together, and were come to him out of every city, he spake by a parable: A sower went out to sow his seed: and as he sowed, some fell by the way side; and it was trodden down, and the fowls of the air devoured it. And some fell upon a rock; and as soon as it was sprung up, it withered away, because it lacked moisture. And some fell among thorns; and the thorns sprang up with it, and choked it. And other fell on good ground, and sprang up, and bare fruit an hundredfold."

To Scott, this meant that good things started small but would flourish in rich soil, just as our relationship was destined to flourish. "I need to get some good soil for us," he said.

I had often talked to Scott about religion and about my faith, and I imagine he was using it to win me back. It was part of his chameleon-like personality. He would be whoever he needed to be to get me.

We kept talking. I reminded him how I felt about honesty. "You know, I could live with the truth. I cannot live a life based on lies, Scott." And I kept pushing him hard, asking him for details, trying to wear him down.

"So if you had nothing to do with her disappearance, Scott, then why can't you tell me about it?" I asked.

"I can tell you everything about the disappearance."

"Okay. Tell me."

"I mean, I went—I went fishing that morning."

"Uh-huh?"

"And, uh—we were supposed to meet up at 4:00."

"Who is we?"

"Laci and I."

"Uh-huh."

"To go to her parents' house for Christmas Eve."

"Uh-huh."

"And, um—I got to the house, and she wasn't there. So I called 'cause I thought she'd be at her parents, and she wasn't there so we immediately started searching."

"Immediately?"

"Yeah. I checked with all the houses around there, and Ron, who is her stepfather, called the hospital. And we went down into the park where she normally walks in case something happened to her there."

I had heard all of this before. It was a little too pat. It was the story he had already shared with the police.

Then I asked him straight out whether Laci had known about our relationship.

"Yes," he said.

This didn't quite compute, so I made him repeat it: "I'm saying now, was Laci aware of the situation about me?"

"Yes."

"She was?"

"Yeah."

"Really? How did she respond about it?"

"Fine."

"Fine?"

"Yeah."

"An eight-month pregnant woman fine about another woman?!"

"You don't know all the facts, Amber. You don't know all the facts. . . ."

"And she was okay with that, huh? That . . . that makes me . . . That's very hard to believe because I've been in a situation like this before, Scott. . . ."

"Yeah."

"And that person was not okay. She wanted to rip my eyes out."

Sometimes my emotions took over, and the conversation went off in all sorts of strange directions:

"So was I ever going to get a dinner invitation to meet the folks?" I asked him.

"Yeah."

"Huh?"

"Oh, yeah."

"Oh, when? At what point? When?"

"Soon."

"Soon? And how would you introduce me?"

"As 'Amber' . . ."

"You're going to introduce me to your folks as 'Amber'?"

"No, I would introduce you as who you are to me."

"And who am I to you?"

"You are so special to me and so wonderful."

But inevitably I dragged him back to the only

166

My older sister, Ava, and me

My mother and father

of me at eighte

At age twenty, teaching my Aunt Beverly how to crochet

Me at twenty-one years old, in one of the hats I crocheted, during my hippie years

My graduation from Fresno City College, 1997

At age twenty

This photograph was taken on December 6, 2002, when I was at a Christmas party. As I later found out, that was the same day Shawn

At a modeling shoot in 2000.

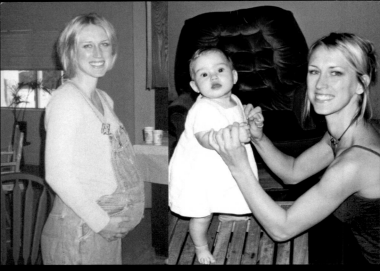

Taken at my baby shower for Ayiana, ten days before she was born

Ayiana and me in the fall of 2001

Celebrating Ayiana's second Fourth of July

Scott getting ready for the formal we went to on December 14, 2002

I had been making this photograph into an ornament for his Christmas

December 24, 02

Dear Scott,

Ayiana is asleep now, it's 10:28 p.m and everything is ready for tomorrow. It has been quite an eventful week already for us. Grandma's with dad, Sis, and family, than Mom's, ect, and tonight my friend Richard invited me for dinner at his friend Tom's house. A very nice family. They remind me of how Shawn's family is. Finally tomorrow ▬▬▬▬▬▬▬ ▬▬▬▬▬▬▬ house and the rest of the family + friends at 2:00 p.m. After I leave their my last stop will be Moises sister's, Diana her husband Tim + two boys than home and life goes back to "normal," what ever that may bee I already miss you, you didn't call like you said you would. I just hope your having a good time w/ your family. Did I muntion that I miss you?

This is a rough draft of a letter I wrote to Scott but never sent.

It's hard for me to believe I'm not going to
be seeing you for another five weeks. That's
roughly 35 day or so. I know it's not that
long but that's already longer than I've know you
now. Do you think you meet someone while
your gone + be tempted? Do you know any women
where you are going that you have an attraction to?
I feel so lost as to? I really don't know what
your world is like. I would like to go to Sac
w/you when you get back and spend some time
on your & grounds and meet your friends too.
My heart hurts when I talk to you on the phone
and I really don't want to be sad or down
when I talk to you. I need to work on that.
I am happy for you that you've got to spend
time w/ your brother + dad + uncle
for Thanksgiving + now your mom + dad
for Christmas. You know I feel sad because
I feel lonely inside and that I wish you
were spending these times with me too!
I don't feel included in your life yet.
I know everything is still new ~~and it already~~
~~got~~ Are things always going to be like
this. you gone + rushing off even on the
phone? ~~Because~~ I need more in my life

I hate not knowing when I'm going to hear
from you agian. How can I deal w/ that (or well)
Not care? That certainly would hurt less!
                                    WORKING ON LOVING you: Amber

MISSING
$500,000 REWARD
For information leading to her safe return

Laci (Rocha) Peterson

Age: 27   Height: 5'1"
Eyes: Brown   Hair: Brown
8 Months Pregnant

Call MODESTO P.D. at 209-342-6166
or visit
lacipeterson.com

Laci was last seen 12/24/02 at 9:30am. She was believed to be headi
toward Dry Creek in Modesto, CA to walk her golden retriever. She was
wearing a white long sleeve shirt and black pants. Laci also has a
sunflower tattoo on her left ankle.

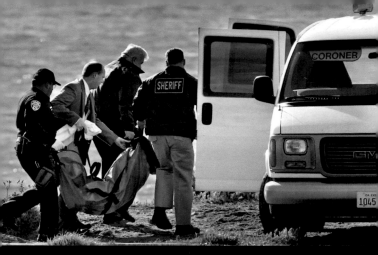

The bodies of Laci Peterson and her unborn son were discovered on April 13 and 14, 2003, near where Scott claimed he had been fishing around the time of Laci's disappearance.

Scott's arrest booking photo, April 18, 2003

With my attorney, Gloria Allred, on the first day of my testimony, August 10, 2004

Scott and his attorney, Mark Geragos

m sketch drawn

subject that mattered: "To me, it's very frustrating to . . . to have this . . . this fear inside my
heart that you had something to do with this
and that you may have possibly and potentially
killed your wife."

"No, you don't need to have that fear. You
know me well enough."

"What was that?"

"I'm not an evil guy . . ."

"Did you love Laci and your baby?"

"I love Laci. I loved Laci, no question."

What did he mean by that? Why was he talking about her in the past tense?

When the conversation ended, Buehler and the
others were quick to sing my praises, but I didn't
feel particularly good about any of it. Where
were the results? At the end of the day, what had
I really accomplished?

I guess I must have looked like a wreck. We
were all sitting at a large conference table, and
every last officer in the room was staring at me.
"Amber," one of them said, "I think we have
enough."

I felt he was only saying that to let me off the
hook. "I want to keep trying," I said. I wanted to
do this for Laci. And I was in a unique position
to do it. I believed I was the only one who might
just have the leverage to discover something important. "I'm all right," I insisted. "And I owe it

to the families to get as much information out of him as I can."

I drove back to Fresno, thinking about everything I'd just been through. I realized there were two Scott Petersons: the one he wanted me to see, and the real one.

Before I went home, I stopped to visit my mother. I remember sitting in front of her computer, digging around to see what else I could learn about the ongoing investigation, making the lie come true, as it were, and discovering that there were many thousands of people all over the world praying for Laci's safe return. I asked God to please listen to them.

A moment later, I came across a photograph of Laci, smiling and pregnant, and I burst into tears. I was becoming unhinged.

That first night back, I took Ayiana and returned to the Bensons', where I felt safe. For a few days, I had no contact with Scott.

On the morning of January 12, very, very early, while it was still dark, I heard noises outside. A moment later, Paul Benson walked into my room.

"Hey," I said, still groggy with sleep.

"Hey."

"What was that noise?"

"Nothing. It was just Lauren, leaving . . ."

"Going to work? At this hour?"

"No," he said, and he looked at me strangely.

"What?" I asked, prodding him.

He took a moment, and stared at me intently. I sensed that he had stronger feelings than I'd realized, and I thought he was about to confess them.

"I want to know how you feel about me, Amber."

Now I was concerned. "I don't know what you mean, Paul. You're like family to me. I love you as a member of my family."

The situation was really uncomfortable. I had thought he and Lauren were the perfect couple. I guess behind closed doors, things are different.

Suddenly I thought of Scott and Laci. They looked like the perfect couple, too, radiant, happy, with that baby on the way, but clearly looks were deceiving. They obviously had their secrets.

Paul was still standing there, just inside the door. "After Ayiana was born," he said, "you turned into this beautiful young mother, so full of love."

I shook my head from side to side. "No, Paul. You're not thinking clearly. You need to deal with your life. You have a family, and your family needs you."

I was crushed. In that instant, I knew I had lost my second family. I had known the Bensons for a decade. It was unthinkable that I wouldn't see them anymore. I was always there. I had never treated Paul as anything other than a beloved uncle. I'd been at their home for Easter, Thanksgiving, Christmas. I was invited to all of their birthdays. But no more. At that moment I knew I would never again be part of their lives.

I packed my bags and took Ayiana and left. I was near tears.

I went to see Shawn in her office because I had to tell her of the feelings I sensed coming from Paul, and I didn't want to wait. She cried. "How will anything make sense to me anymore?" she asked. Months later, when she sent out her wedding invitations, I wasn't on the list. I understood why, and it hurt: I knew our relationship would never be the same again.

I returned home that day feeling more alone and more isolated than ever, and the phone rang. It was Scott. I was feeling incredibly fragile, so I just blurted it out: "Do I need to be afraid of you?"

I *was* afraid of him. For two weeks now, I was afraid every time I approached my house. I was afraid when I opened my front door. I was afraid when I walked into my bedroom. Even now, when I think back on it, I shudder. And to think that I had almost given my heart to this sociopath.

"Absolutely not," Scott said. "I am not a monster."

"I never said you were, Scott," I said, pointedly. Then, just as pointedly, I asked him the question that was on everyone's mind: "Did you have anything to do with your wife's disappearance?"

"Uh, uh . . . No. But I know who did, and I'll tell you later when I see you."

I felt such anger inside me. I was sick of all the lies. I kept thinking back to those first few days, when he made me feel as if the relationship held so much promise. "Is it written all over me, you know, 'sucker' or something?!"

Next thing I knew, I was interrogating Scott about his last night with Laci: "So you watched the movie together? And then you went to sleep together or went to bed together, right? Where did you sleep?"

"In a bed," he replied.

"You went to separate beds to go to sleep, then?"

"I can't say yes or no to that," he said.

"Why?"

"Because those are details that we can't talk about now."

I was really frustrated at this point, and I told him so in no uncertain words. "This has been an unbelievable mindfuck."

* * *

171

On January 15, three weeks into the investigation, the police went to see Laci's family. They told them that Scott had been having an affair with another woman, me, and that he had taken out a $250,000 life insurance policy on his wife.

Two days later, Scott called, whining: "Laci's family is accusing me of having something to do with it now. . . . That's why I wanted to call. I just wanted to make sure you're not being bothered. "

"Not yet," I said, ice cold.

"I hope you aren't."

"You know, I—I had Detective Buehler calling me today, asking where I was on the 23rd and 24th. . . ."

Buehler had told me it was just a formality, and I knew I wasn't a suspect, but I wasn't above trying to push Scott's buttons.

"Oh my God!" he exclaimed.

"Um, let's see what else? I guess at six, something's coming on with Laci Peterson's family. They are going to make a statement of some sort. I have no idea what."

"Yeah. I heard (about) that press conference."

"So what is your take on all this, Scott?"

"I'm just . . . The only thing I mean . . . I just feel bad . . . I just hope you're not bothered anymore by any of this."

"It's a little late for that, Scott."

"Yeah, I know, but I can hope."

"You can hope? You can hope for a lot of

things. I mean, you can hope for your Laci to return; you can hope that I'm not bothered; you can hope that the news coverage only focuses on her. You can hope all these things, Scott, but the fact is—truth prevails. . . ."

"The truth will prevail, and that's why we're confident," he said.

"When? When? And why—why does it have to take so long . . . ? They're asking me where I was on the 23rd. You've heard things. 'Maybe the girlfriend was involved.'"

"No."

"Great! Where was I on the 23rd? Now I've got to wrack my brain. Where was I on the 23rd? Most likely with my daughter . . ."

"Yeah."

"Where was Scott?" I said, still pushing. "Where was Scott on the 23rd? Where was Laci on the 23rd? Can you answer me that?"

There was no answer.

"Hello? Hello?" I heard a silence, and I heard a breath. "Did you hear me?"

"Yeah, I did," he said. "Oh—are you asking me?"

"You obviously didn't hear me because I asked a question."

"No. I wasn't really sure if you were really asking me where I was on the 23rd."

"Yeah. Where were you on the 23rd? And where was Laci?"

"I was at work," he said, and he repeated it: "I was at work."

"She wasn't with you all day . . . ?"

"Amber," he said finally, relenting and asking the obvious: "Are you asking if I had something to do with this?"

"You never told me you haven't."

"Yes, I have. I had nothing to do with this. You know that."

"How . . . How . . . How am I supposed to know that when I didn't even know you were currently married, you have a child on the way, how was I supposed to know . . . ? How am I supposed to know that you have nothing to do with this? Tell me that, Scott?"

"You know, you know, Amber, I know that you're intuitive enough to know."

"Then explain all the coincidences and . . . and lies you've told me."

"I lied to you. You're right . . . I'm sorry, Amber. I'm sorry I lied to you. I'm sorry you're involved in this. I hope you're not—"

"You didn't answer the question, Scott . . . You're deferring."

"What was your question? What was your question?"

"I said, with all these things, how can I not possibly think you have something to do with this?"

"The only way you can know that is by . . . the only way . . . "

"You lied about having a girlfriend, you lied to me about having a wife."

"The only way is that you know me well enough to know that I could never do anything like this."

"I don't know you well enough. How could I possibly know you well enough . . . ? I . . . I . . ."

"I think you know. I think you know me. You know people's hearts and souls, Amber. Better than anyone in this world, you know people."

"And from what I know, Scott, and this pains me to say, this was all a plan . . . "

"Amber, it just hurts so bad for you to think I could have something to do with this."

I lost my cool again: "What a mistake there, huh? On my part. What a fool. That's why I said you make me feel like such a fool, Scott."

"I'm sorry, Amber. You're not a fool. I never should . . . I'm sorry you're going through this."

"Never should have what, Scott? Finish your sentence. Never should have what?"

"Never should have become involved with you."

"No, you should not have. You're married."

"Yeah."

"Why did you? I mean that question: Why did you call me when Shawn told you if you are not serious about anyone, especially my friend Amber, she's been through enough, don't call her. Why did you call me?"

"I don't know."

" 'I don't know' is not good enough for me, Scott. I deserve an answer."

"That's all I have, Amber."

"You have the answer. Give it to me."

I was angry, bordering on furious. Scott was the only one who knew the truth, he was the only one with the answers, and we were all waiting on him. I wanted an answer. I felt I *deserved* it. But I got nothing from him. Nothing.

On January 20, Scott called to tell me that he had hired a private investigator, and that one of the first things his investigator discovered was that *The National Enquirer* already had an investigator on the case, trying to dig up dirt on Scott and possibly on me. He sounded unnerved.

For the next few days, our contact was limited. Then on January 22 I got a call from Detective Buehler, asking if I'd be good enough to go to the Modesto Police Department for a polygraph. I told him I didn't have a problem with that, and I agreed to drive up the next day.

Buehler was waiting for me at the Modesto station, and he introduced me to the woman who would be administering the test. She had me fill out a questionnaire, and went over the questions with me, and she took the time to assure me that there would be no surprises. "There's no hidden agenda here," she said.

She put sensors on my chest, my arms, and one of my fingers, and the test got under way. She began by asking me my name. She asked if I'd ever hit anyone. She wanted to know if I knew where Laci was, and whether I'd had anything to do with her disappearance. It was more nerve-wracking than I'd expected.

At one point, she had me write a number on a piece of paper. I wrote the number "8." She told me to lie to her so that the polygraph could gauge my response, and when she asked me if I'd written the number "8" I said no.

The whole thing took about two hours, and when we were done Buehler asked if he could take a few hair samples. I had to yank out several clumps. From the top of my head; from the side of my head; and even from the nape of my neck. It wasn't fun.

I found out later that some unidentified hairs had been found in Scott's truck, and they wanted determine if they were mine. For a moment, I wondered if there had been other women in his life, and how many, and whether he'd been seeing them while he was seeing me.

Scott called again. He was concerned about me and asked me how I felt. "I feel sickened," I said. "I feel betrayed."

"Yeah?"

"Sad. Don't know what's real. It's hard for me sometimes to close my eyes."

"Really? What happens when you do?"

"My mind just wanders," I said.

"To what?"

"A million different things."

"Yeah?"

"I don't feel like this is real," I said. "I don't feel like this is happening."

"Yeah," he said.

I asked him how he felt, and he said he'd been through a whole range of emotions. "A roller coaster . . . I mean, every day . . . Everything from anger to, you know, I feel, you know, such guilt that I involved you in this and such anger toward whoever it could be, you know, who abducted Laci. And, you know, sadness on both sides and a little bit of hope . . . Well, a *lot* of hope. So I'm just like you. Just a range of emotions." Then he added that I was "much more a victim" than he was.

"How is that?" I asked. "How am I more a victim than you?"

"Well, because, you know, you are . . . Well, obviously Laci was the largest victim. But you, you know, you didn't have to be involved in this situation except that, you know, I want . . . I was seeing you."

I didn't think to ask why he thought Laci was

the "largest" victim; nothing had been determined at that point. And I guess I didn't think to ask because I was upset all over again. "I don't understand why you called me," I said, remembering the beginning of our nightmarish relationship. "You haven't taken care of your shit yet. You're still married. When I asked you after you told me you lost your wife, I said, 'Are you ready for me?' And you said, 'Absolutely. O God, yes.' Or whatever you said. I mean how . . . I don't understand how you could have said that when you weren't ready for me. You're still married and have a child on the way. I mean, that just blows my mind. If you were ready for me, then you would have . . . this relationship—you wouldn't have . . ." I was having trouble catching my breath. "You wouldn't have been married. You wouldn't have been running off to go see your wife . . . This is not the way . . . It's not right, *was* not right . . . You take care of your shit before you involve somebody else!"

I had been watching the news more attentively, and in recent days I had seen clips of people at the volunteer center, and of course Laci's friends and family had talked about her and about Scott and about the two of them together. And I couldn't help myself. I told Scott how difficult it was to listen to them, to hear them talk about their "wonderful" relationship.

"Yeah," he said, absently.

"And you had a perfect marriage."

"I'm sorry, I missed that," he said. "Say it again."

"I said it's frustrating to hear—"

"I know, I know, baby," he said, cutting me off. And he was gone.

The next day, early, I woke to the ringing phone. It was the owner of American Body Works. He said that the morning DJ at a local radio station was doing a live interview with one of the women from work, and that I should probably tune in. I turned on the radio and heard her talking about me and my relationship with Scott— the little she knew about us, anyway. She even disclosed that I'd been crocheting a scarf for Scott. This was tremendously upsetting, but at least she hadn't mentioned me by name. That didn't happen till later in the day, on another program. . . .

I got Ayiana out of bed and took her to school, then hurried to work. As soon as I got done with my first client, a colleague told me that a reporter from CBS had been calling incessantly, trying to get me on the phone. I refused to take his call, so he sent a note. He said he could make arrangements to fly me to New York, and that he'd put me and my "son" up in a five-star hotel, and that the network would protect me from the coming "media circus." He was wrong about my having a son, but he wasn't wrong about the coming media circus. By midday, I was drowning in messages from reporters, all of them looking for the scoop of the day.

I hid out in my small, windowless massage room, refusing to talk to any of them. Shortly after one, Dave Markovich showed up with lunch. "I feel like I'm in a state of siege," I told him.

After six hours of this, the Modesto police decided to come to the rescue. They came to the office and hustled me through the back to a waiting squad car, and they proceeded to drive me home. A very persistent reporter followed in an SUV, and I realized that things were going to get a lot worse before they got better.

En route, one of the officers reached Buehler and broached the idea of having me make a general statement to the press. Everyone seemed to think this was a good idea, so I went along with it. I spoke to Buehler on the phone. "My hair's a mess and all my makeup is back in my car, which I had to leave in the parking lot," I said. "I'm wearing a borrowed men's jacket over a T-shirt. I'd like to go home and at least change into some decent clothes. I'm a mess."

"Just pull your hair back," he said. "You look nice with your hair pulled back."

"I don't normally wear it that way," I said.

"Even better. When you're out in public, people won't recognize you."

That didn't even register.

When we got to my house, a female officer accompanied me inside and waited while I got ready. I put my hair up, per Buehler's suggestion, and over-sprayed it by mistake. It looked frightful, but there was nothing I could do. We went back to the car and left for Modesto.

I tried to stay calm during the trip, but my phone kept ringing. Scott called a couple of times, but I didn't answer. I didn't have the recorder with me, and I didn't want to miss what he had to say—today of all days.

As soon as we arrived in Modesto, I started getting pretty nervous. A couple of officers, including Doug Ridenour, began to help me prepare a statement. Meanwhile, their public relations department got busy contacting all the appropriate news outlets in the area. Before long, a regular battalion had begun to gather in the press room.

"I'm nervous," I said.

"I can understand that," Ridenour said. "But hang tough. We'll get you in and out of there fast. It'll be over before you know it."

I still couldn't believe I was going to go through with this. I don't really think I understood until that moment the degree to which this case had captured the country's collective imagination. But it was suddenly starting to sink in. Scott and Laci looked like the perfect, all-American couple. Scott was handsome, charming, successful. Laci was the prototypical girl-next-door, glowing with life. But looks were deceiving, clearly. And I myself had been badly deceived. I think that the deception, too, was part of the story's appeal. Women across the country would look at Scott and think, *I could have fallen for that guy*. Well, I *had* fallen for him. I'd started out full of hope, and now here I was, trapped in a nightmare beyond my imagination.

When the time came for me to face the cameras, I was practically hyperventilating. Then, to compound matters, as we were making our way down the corridor, my cell phone rang. It was Scott. I didn't take the call. I braced myself and kept moving, with Ridenour and Buehler setting the pace on either side of me.

We went in—I couldn't believe the number of reporters who'd shown up—and everyone fell silent. Ridenour whispered that I should wait on the sidelines. He moved toward the bank of microphones and told the packed room that earlier in the day a member of the press had made my name public, and he confirmed that I'd been having a relationship with Scott Peterson. He pointed out that, until very recently, I had not known Scott was married, and said he hoped that everyone would be good enough to respect my privacy. I was going to make a brief statement, he said, but I would not be taking questions.

At that point, Ridenour looked at me, and—for a moment—I was just absolutely frozen. Then I pulled myself together and approached the microphone and cleared my throat.

"Okay, first of all, I met Scott Peterson on November 20th of 2002. I was introduced to him. I was told he was unmarried. Scott told me he was not married. We did have a romantic relationship.

"When I discovered he was involved in the Laci Peterson disappearance case, I immediately contacted the Modesto Police Department.

"Although I could have sold the photos of Scott and I to the tabloids, I knew this was not the right thing to do. For fear of jeopardizing the case or the investigation, I will not comment further."

I had more to say, but I almost couldn't get it out. I felt dangerously close to tears. Everyone was staring at me. For a split second, I thought I was going to black out. But Ridenour came to my rescue. He was standing just behind me, to my left, and he leaned close and whispered that I'd done a beautiful job. I took a deep, bracing breath and finished what I had to say:

"I am very sorry for Laci's family, and the pain

that this has caused them. And I pray for her safe return, as well.

"I would appreciate (if) my friends and acquaintances (would) refrain from talking about me to the media for profit or recognition. I am a single mother with a twenty-three-month-old child, and I ask [you] to respect my privacy. Thank you."

I turned and moved off. I knew I hadn't quite nailed it, but I hoped my message had been clear.

Ridenour went back to the microphones: "Amber Frey had contacted the Modesto Police Department on Monday, December 30th, 2002," he said. "She met with detectives and gave the information about the relationship with Scott Peterson. This information was verified by a variety of means, and Amber Frey has been cooperative in the investigation.

"For the near future, we've asked Ms. Frey not to make any statements to the media. It's her desire that you respect her privacy. Please don't follow, harass, or make any other attempts to interview her during the investigation."

As I retreated to the sidelines, Ridenour was peppered with questions. He was asked whether I had told police where Scott was on Christmas Eve, and whether I had provided details that tied Scott to Laci's disappearance. And he was asked how they had eliminated me as a suspect. He was evasive about the first couple of questions, but he addressed this last one: "The investigators have a variety of ways that they've been able to eliminate her from the investigation."

They never told me how they had eliminated me from the investigation, but I got the impression from Detective Buehler that they had been paying close attention to every detail of the telephone calls. It occurred to me that if I had had something to hide, those conversations would have put me at risk. I obviously had nothing to hide. I was honest and forthright, and I was doing my best to help them with their case.

At one point, one of the reporters asked whether I had called the police because I had learned of Laci's disappearance, or whether I had contacted them because I found out that he was married. The gist of the question was unmistakable: Had I called to try to help them, or was I involved as the wrathful other woman?

"Her statement, I believe, said that she did not know that Scott was married at the time that they had this relationship," Ridenour said. "That was her statement."

When Ridenour was done, Modesto Police Chief Roy Wasden took the microphone and thanked the reporters for their help. They kept shouting out their questions and before long had worked their way back to me. "We're not going to discuss Amber," Wasden said forcefully.

"Amber gave you her statement. You have the information that Amber was comfortable sharing with you. She's asked to have her privacy respected. We are going to do that. I'm not going to comment about Amber, her private life, where she works, where she lives—any of those things. Amber wants to be able to get on with her life."

After the conference, Buehler took me aside and told me that three of Laci's friends were there and wanted to talk to me. I was a little nervous, but Buehler escorted me to a private room and made the introductions. All three women thanked me for coming forward and for what I'd done. "If you were new to Laci's neighborhood, she would have been the first person on the block to invite you over," one of them said. It made me feel like crying.

A moment later, we turned to watch the broadcast of the news conference. There was a small television in the room, and someone had turned it on. When I saw myself on the small screen, I realized just how nervous I'd been, and how awful I looked, and I was very glad that it was over. I had absolutely no idea what lay in store for me.

In the middle of the broadcast, a phone rang. It was Laci's mother, Sharon Rocha. She had been watching the broadcast and called the precinct, hoping to reach me before I left. I took the phone. Mrs. Rocha introduced herself and thanked me for coming forward. She said she would like to meet me at some point, maybe the next day, if I was comfortable with the idea. I told her that I would be honored to meet her, thanked her for her kind words, and told her I was praying for her and Laci.

It was late by this time, and I didn't relish the long trip back to Fresno. One of Laci's friends, Lori Ellsworth, a woman of about my age, invited me to spend the night at her place, and I gratefully accepted. We stayed up late, talking about Laci and Scott and about our own lives. Lori had a stack of newspapers and magazines at her place, going back to the beginning of Laci's disappearance. I reiterated that I had never had any idea that Scott was married, as if trying to absolve myself, and she said she never doubted it, not even for a moment. "I know he lied to Laci," she said. "I wonder how many other lies he told her during the marriage. That smug bastard."

She showed me pictures of Laci I had never seen, and there were moments when she was moved to tears. I was exhausted by this time. It had been a very long day. I just needed a bed.

I think I was asleep before my head even touched the pillow.

The next morning, Lori took me to meet Laci's mother. Mrs. Rocha was incredibly gracious, and clearly in great pain. There were photographs of

Laci all over the house and even one of Laci and Scott together, which surprised me, given the circumstances. Mrs. Rocha said she was hoping to fill in some gaps in her own thinking, and wondered if she could ask me a few questions. She asked me when I first met Scott, and she asked me for specific dates. "I'm sorry," she said. "I'm not trying to put you on the spot. I'm just trying to get this clear in my own head."

From time to time she would refer to her desk calendar, thinking back, trying to make sense of the past few weeks. But of course none of it made sense.

I met Laci's sister, and her aunt, and her step-father, Ron Grantski. They were all incredibly kind to me. "I hand it to you for doing the right thing," Grantski said.

Before long, the house was filled with Laci's friends and relatives. Everyone was so support-ive and so kind that I began to cry. "I can't be-lieve I'm sitting here with all of you, with Laci's friends and family," I said, tears pouring down my face. "I have been so alone and isolated. Thank you for this. And thank you for being so understanding."

It took a huge weight off my shoulders, just knowing that they knew that I wasn't the enemy. But in another way, that visit broke my heart. When I looked into the eyes of the people who knew Laci best, I saw something I didn't want to see: a group of people who desperately loved Laci, and who were beginning to suspect that she wasn't coming home.

It was during this visit that I also got a more complete picture of the real Laci, the Laci the press didn't know. She and her older brother, Brent, started life on a dairy farm, west of Escalon, but their parents divorced when they were young, and they moved to Modesto with their mother. To Laci, Modesto must have seemed like a big city. She went to Sonoma Elementary School and made friends who were still in her life at the time she disappeared.

If there was a common theme during my short visit, it was the way everyone spoke about Laci's huge, wonderful smile. Even Laci's mother talked about it, saying what an incredibly happy baby she had been. "Every morning, she woke up with a smile on her face."

People said Laci's smile lit up a room. They said she had boundless energy, and a real zest for life. And one of her favorite things was plants, which she had loved from her days on the farm. It was no surprise, then, that when it was time for college she went to California Polytechnic State University, in San Luis Obispo, to study horticulture.

Then she met and fell in love with Scott Peterson, and—for a time—they looked like the happiest couple in the world.

People knew better now, but they didn't want to talk about that. They were too fragile. And maybe still hopeful.

At the time, I didn't realize that the previous day, just hours before my press conference, Laci's friends and family had given a press conference of their own. Laci's younger half-sister, Amy Rocha, had been the first to speak. "The past few weeks have been the most painful I've ever experienced," she had said, and couldn't go on. Then Laci's older brother, Brent, took the microphone. He said the family had been informed about Scott's affair, and noted that he had lost faith in him. "I trusted him and stood by him in the initial phases of my sister's disappearance. However, Scott has not been forthcoming with information regarding my sister's disappearance, and I'm only left to question what else he may be hiding."

Sharon Rocha was the last to speak. The following day, when I read her words in the newspaper, I wept.

"Since Christmas Eve, our one and only focus has been to find Laci and bring her home to us," she told the assembled reporters. "I love my daughter so much. I miss her every minute of every day. I miss seeing her. I miss our talking together. I miss listening to the excitement in her voice when she talks to me about her baby. I miss not being able to share with her the anticipation of her approaching delivery date. I miss listening to her talk about her future with her husband and her baby. I miss sharing our thoughts and our lives together. I miss her smile and her laughter and her sense of humor. And I miss everything about her.

"Someone has taken all of this away from me and everyone else who loves her. There are no words that can possibly describe the ache in my heart, or the emptiness in my life."

I was back home by now, reading this account in the paper, when Scott called. I wiped my tears and hooked up the recorder. "I just wanted to say that how brave you were," Scott said, launching right in, "and I'm really glad that you . . . that you did that." He was referring to the news conference.

"It wasn't a matter of choice," I replied.

"What's that?"

"It really wasn't a matter of choice. They were staked out at my work all day."

"I know, but it's still incredibly brave. It just shows what amazing character you have. . . . You're, uh, just amazing, just unbelievable. . . ."

I thought *he* was unbelievable. I didn't know what to say to him. I had never dealt with anyone like Scott Peterson in my life.

At one point, Ayiana walked into the room.

The TV was on, and the station was running a clip of the news conference. "Mama is on TV!" she squealed. "My mom is on TV!"

In the days ahead, I was recognized everywhere I went. People would stop me on the street to thank me for coming forward and for having the courage to speak up. I was also contacted by the press, who seemed tireless, and at one point I called Buehler to tell him what was going on. "They keep offering me gifts and luxury hotels and telling me that if I give them an exclusive the rest of the pack will leave me alone," I said.

Buehler said it was my call, but he also said something else—and it went a long way toward helping me make up my mind: "We'd prefer to try the case in court," he noted, "not in public."

The reporters kept calling, and I kept turning them down. That didn't stop them, though. *The National Enquirer* was quick to describe me as Scott's "mistress." This was patently unfair, not to mention painful. I hadn't known Scott was married. I'd been lied to. I would never willingly become anybody's mistress.

That same week, I received a handwritten note from Connie Chung, and we spoke on the phone the following day. She wanted what everyone else wanted: *An Exclusive Interview with Amber Frey.* I told her I didn't want any publicity, and that I just wanted to get on with my life, but that I'd speak to Sharon Rocha first to see how she felt about it. Connie Chung commended me for taking the family's feelings into account. "Believe it or not," she said, "most people wouldn't be that considerate." Then she told me that if I *did* decide to talk to her, she wanted me to stay with her, at her place in Manhattan, and that I should bring Ayiana.

The next day, I talked to Sharon Rocha and told her about my conversation with Connie Chung. She said she didn't think it would benefit the case and suggested I try to limit my conversations about it to the police. I agreed with her, and told her so, and I thanked her for her advice. She thanked me for calling. "I don't want to do anything to jeopardize the investigation," I said.

In the days ahead, I followed the case, though not as avidly as much of the rest of the country. I read in *The Modesto Bee* that Scott had laughed and smiled during a vigil for Laci. I heard that Scott had traded in Laci's Land Rover and had used the money to buy a new truck for himself. His other truck had been seized as evidence.

I read that one of the neighbors had been struck by the fact that the curtains at the Peterson home remained tightly shut on Christmas Eve and Christmas Day. And I read that another neighbor reported having seen Scott loading something heavy into the back of his truck around the time Laci vanished. It made me think of that green lockbox I'd seen on our first date, and the thought made me shudder.

In the midst of this, Scott gave an interview to Gloria Gomez, a local television reporter.

"Take a look at my hand," he told her at one point. "You can see cuts here on my knuckles, numerous scars. I work on farms. I work with machinery. I know I cut my knuckle on that day . . . on Christmas Eve . . . reaching in the toolbox in my truck and then into the pocket on the door. I cut open my knuckle, and there was a bloodstain on the door."

I suddenly remembered a conversation I'd had with Scott shortly after the police went to search his house. He was worried about the way the police could twist any little thing against him. "It could be, you know, the smallest thing," he said. "I mean, you know . . . the police asked me about cuts on my hands."

"Uh-huh," I said, curious.

"You know . . . I always have cuts on my hands. . . . I may have blood in my truck, and they say it could be something like that."

"Are you in pain?" I had asked him. "On any kind of medications right now?"

"No," he said. "But obviously it's scary. But it's not the important thing. . . ."

"So with all . . . with all of, you know, finding

the blood and everything, what have they come back to you on that?"

"Nothing's come back," he had said. "They took my car and they, you know, they called me up and they're like 'Why is there blood on your door?'"

"And why was there blood on your door?"

"Because I cut my finger on the door driving home. I have a big ol' scratch on my knuckle."

"How would—how can you get a scratch like . . . ? I don't understand how that happens."

"I was reaching in the pocket of the door of the truck."

"Uh-huh?"

"And opened up an old scab on my knuckle."

"What was this old scab from?"

"Just from working. From scraping off the woodworking . . ."

At one point during the television interview, Gloria Gomez flat out asked him about his relationship with me. "Did Laci find out about the affair, or did you just come out and tell her?" she wondered.

"No, I informed her about it. I don't believe she knew."

"Why come out?" Gomez persisted. "I mean, what made you say, 'I'm gonna tell her today.' What made that day the day to tell her?"

"Just because it was the right thing to do," Scott said.

Then she asked him about the $250,000 insurance policy he had taken out on Laci's life. "We have life insurance policies in place that were established when we bought this home you're in right now, two years ago," Scott said.

His emotions were all over the place, and on a couple occasions he looked close to tears, but he got angry when Gomez began to ask him about the police investigation. "I'm not going to waste what little time we have . . . by defending myself about irrelevant things," he said. He further asked her to back off: "We're starting to go into areas that investigators have asked me not to comment about. So we should probably simply put the brakes on." Ms. Gomez later talked to the police and learned that he had lied about that, too. They told her that they had been glued to the interview, eager to hear everything he had to say, and actually *hoping* he would talk. They had never asked him to keep silent.

For some strange reason, however, he decided to tell Gomez the truth about me. "Yes, she did not know—she did not know that I was married," he said in response to a direct question. "That is correct, um, so I'm glad she came forward. . . . I informed her, um, that I am married and of Laci's disappearance shortly after, um, Christmas Eve. . . . I don't know the exact date."

On January 28, Diane Sawyer aired an interview with Scott on *Good Morning America*. Scott told Sawyer that he and Laci had a "glorious" marriage. . . . "She was amazing—*is* amazing," he said, correcting himself.

When she asked him about his unborn child, noting that he hadn't mentioned him, Scott appeared to be struggling with his emotions. He claimed it was too hard for him to go into the baby's room. "That door is closed until there's someone to put in there," he said.

His feelings for me were clearly not as intense as his feelings for his unborn child. When Diane Sawyer asked him, point-blank, whether he was in love with me, Scott didn't even have to think about it: "No," he said. "I'd have to say that I respect her, and as I imagine everyone does after seeing her come out and do the press conference. . . . What an amazing character she has."

Under further questioning, he insisted that his affair with me wasn't anything that would have broken his marriage apart, and he claimed that he had told the police about us immediately after Laci disappeared. This was patently untrue. I'm the one who told them about our relationship. Scott didn't acknowledge it until after my news conference in Modesto.

Scott also repeated what he had told Gloria Gomez: that he had come clean about the affair with Laci. "It was not positive, obviously, you know, it was inappropriate," he said. "But it was not something that we weren't dealing with . . ."

"Do you really expect people to believe that an eight-and-a-half-month pregnant woman learns her husband has had an affair and is saintly and casual about it, accommodating, makes a peace with it?" Sawyer asked.

"No one knows our relationship but us," Scott said.

No, Scott. No one knows but you. And no one ever will know.

At one point, Sawyer said: "I think everybody at home wants the answer to the same question: 'Did you murder your wife?'"

To which Scott responded: "No. No. I did not. And I had absolutely nothing to do with her disappearance. And you use the word murder and right now everyone is looking for a body. And that is the hardest thing because that is not a possible resolution for us. To use the word murder and—yes, and that is a possibility. It's not one we're ready to accept, and it creeps in my mind late at night and early in the morning and during the day all we can think about is the right resolution to find her." He later went on to say, "Violence towards women is unapproachable. . . . It is the most disgusting act, to me."

Scott called me later that evening to find out if I'd seen the interview. I told him I had; that I'd seen part of it, anyway.

"Yeah, they really hacked out a lot of stuff I said on most things."

"What was that?" I asked.

"They hacked out a lot of stuff I said about a lot of things. . . . So hopefully they'll . . . They're going to do more tomorrow, so hopefully that one's better. . . ."

"Are you doing another interview as well?"

"No, no. I just sat down with her for two or three hours yesterday. And uh, I think they're going to strain it into three parts."

"Oh, really?"

"Yeah."

"Scott," I said after a moment of silence, "there are a few things that . . . that bothered me about your interview, if I could talk to you about it."

"Sure."

"I guess . . . I guess the one that bothered me the most was when they asked if you are in love with me and you said no. Right?"

"Yeah. I thought that might bother you."

The fact is—and I mean this from the bottom of my heart—it hadn't bothered me. When I first heard it, it had an abruptness that felt like a slap in the face. But as soon as I regained my composure, I realized that it hadn't really affected me. There was nothing Scott Peterson could do to me that could touch me in any fundamental way.

He was still going on about it, defending himself. "(T)hat's one of the things they cut down really bad on what I had continued to say."

"What? Okay—what was that, then? What did they cut down?"

"Well, you could see the . . . there was a skip from when I answered 'no' to when I said, you know, that I respected you. Um . . . and they cut out, you know, the parts that I mentioned that I care about you and I, you know, hope the media doesn't continue to harass you and you don't deserve, you know, that type of thing so that's basically what I said and they cut it down to um . . . what was a very quick 'no' and then the respect thing . . . Um . . . it was a very fast 'no' because I was coached . . . Um, you know, they just kept saying 'you should say no,' 'you should say no,' 'you should say no.' And I know I, you know, I said 'no' so fast and then they cut out the rest of it. . . ."

All of this waffling gave me an idea: I told Scott I was deeply confused by all of his lies, and I asked him if he'd take a polygraph for me. I had heard the same rumor everyone else had heard, a rumor that even Diane Sawyer had asked him about—specifically, that the police had suggested he take a polygraph, and that he had refused—and I told him it would go a long way to clearing things up.

Scott had the gall to tell me he had already taken it, which I knew to be a lie, so I asked him to take another one, "for me . . . We had something good going, Scott. And maybe we could have something good going again if you help me rebuild that trust. Taking that polygraph could be an important first step in that direction."

"Okay," he said finally. "I'll do it. But you'll have to come with me."

I told him I didn't know whether that was possible, that the police wouldn't allow it, and he said he would arrange to have an independent company administer the test. "The police are already way too biased," he explained.

When I got off the phone, I called Buehler and told him what had happened. He knew I was just trying to help push the investigation along, and he said he appreciated my efforts, but he refused to let me take part in the scheme. "I don't want you anywhere near that guy," he said. "He's dangerous."

Now I knew what Buehler had been unwilling to put into words: that he thought what everyone else was thinking; that Laci and her unborn child were dead, and that Scott had killed them.

"Couldn't you guys protect me?" I said, still wanting to help.

"Amber," he said gravely. "It would be over in a matter of seconds." Then he added: "And your daughter only has you."

On January 31, the media picked up a story about Laci having been spotted in a store somewhere in Washington State, and apparently there was an image of her on a surveillance tape.

"Well, I have to go to Washington to get those tapes," Scott said.

"Okay, when are you going to Washington?"

"What's that?"

"When are you going to Washington?"

"I don't know," he said, sounding less than interested. "I'd have to get in contact with the police there and see if they would let me look at 'em."

"It's just—the story doesn't sound right," I said.

"I know, but I need to know. And I'll look at 'em and I need to find out if it is her."

By the time Scott got around to calling the Washington State Police, a couple of days later, they'd already concluded that there was nothing to story.

The next day, February 1, Scott called to say he had set up the polygraph. He gave me the name of a place and an address and told me to meet him there in a couple of hours. I didn't believe any of this, and I had no intention of going, but when I got off the phone I called the place and was surprised to discover that it was a legitimate company. "Is Scott Peterson scheduled to come in for a polygraph?" I asked.

"Yes," I was told. "He said he was just waiting

to hear from the person who would be coming with him."

I got off the phone and called Buehler, and he said I was doing the right thing by not going. Meanwhile, Scott was en route to the place, with Al Brocchini tailing him. When he arrived, he spotted Brocchini, and he went up to his car, angry, and demanded to know whether I'd tipped him off. Brocchini said nothing, and Scott stormed away.

"You set me up!" he told me on the phone moments later, near tears.

"No, Scott. I had nothing to do with it."

He was sobbing by this time, and we either lost the call or he hung up. I called Lori Ellsworth, up in Modesto, to tell her what had happened. I felt bad and wanted to hear a friendly voice. I also knew I could speak openly to Laci's friends, since none of them had sold their stories to the tabloids. "I'm here anytime you need me, Amber," she told me. I felt instantly better.

The next thing I knew, Brocchini was at my front door. I was still in my pajamas. "Please tell me you're not planning on seeing Peterson," he said. I noticed a couple of news vans out on the street. I don't know whether they had followed Brocchini, but clearly they thought something big was about to happen. "I never had any intention of seeing Scott," I replied.

"Good," he said, and he left.

I was mad. Not only because the press was there, but because I was going to be forced to win back Scott's confidence. I must have called Buehler twenty times in the next hour, venting and screaming. I didn't want Scott to think I had set him up—by this time, I, too, was convinced that he was dangerous—and I didn't like the fact that Brocchini had inadvertently led the media to my door. Buehler did his best to calm me down, but I was still a wreck, so I called my friend Dave Markovich and asked him to come over.

"I don't want to be alone," I said.

Dave was there within half an hour, and he spent the night.

Months later, I learned from the newspapers that the police had been bugging Scott's phones, and that they put a stop to it at around this time. Apparently, they felt they had everything they needed. I didn't know that they had tapped his line, just as I didn't know that they had put a tracking device on his new truck. When I finally found out, Buehler told me that the tracking device had been put there, in part, to keep me safe. "We didn't want him anywhere near you," he explained. "We were ready to move in if he got too close."

On February 7, Scott called, sobbing. "We just need to see each other, Amber, at least for a couple of hours."

I didn't want to see him, but I didn't want to be unnecessarily cruel, so I simply told him we couldn't risk it. If the police weren't following him, the media were, and I told him it wouldn't look right, especially at this critical juncture in the investigation. He said we could meet at the home of a friend of his, in Lake Arrowhead, and he assured me that it was safe, but I still said no. I had no intention of driving to an isolated mountain cabin in the middle of the night to meet Scott Peterson, but I needed to let him down gently. I wanted Scott to trust me. I still hoped something good would come of these painfully trying conversations. I had seen despair in the eyes of Laci's friends and families, and I knew that even Buehler had joined the ranks of those who thought Laci was dead. I continued to refuse to believe it. I still had hope. I was praying that Scott would break down and lead me to Laci.

The next time we spoke, I told him that I had many questions for him, and that they were keeping me up at night.

"You know all the answers to the things you want to know," he said.

I was suddenly hopeful. I thought this might be the first crack in the veneer. "I do?" I asked.

"Yes," he said.

"I do?" I repeated.

"Yes."

"How do I know?"

"I wish I could tell you, but you've guessed the answers to all of them."

"How do I have the answers, Scott?"

"Well, you don't have the answers, but you've guessed at them and you know them and it's just going to take time and trust for me to—not trust—but time for me to be able to tell you."

Later, I reflected on the call. Scott's tone was different. There was less energy in him. His words hadn't felt as rehearsed as they sometimes did. There was even a hint of desperation in his voice, and, oddly enough, it gave me hope.

I thought that maybe, finally, I was going to learn something useful.

••••••••••••••••••••

"Good-bye for now."

On February 9, *The National Enquirer* published a number of the nude photographs I'd posed for years earlier, when I had tried my hand at modeling. I had never even seen them myself; had never even gone back to the studio to look at them. Now they were on the newsstands across the nation, on public display, and I felt utterly humiliated. I suspected that this was the work of the *Enquirer* reporters who had been hounding me from the start.

The following day, one of the networks decided to capitalize on the *Enquirer* story, and they kept flashing my pictures throughout the broadcast. When Scott called, I was beside myself. "I couldn't . . . I . . . I cannot believe how much she . . . this program kept showing my picture," I said. "My heart's pounding right now. I'm still so furious. . . ."

"That's disgusting," he said. "I'm so sorry, Amber."

I felt ridiculed and belittled by the media. I had been doing everything in my power to help the investigation, and I just wanted to get through it, but they were standing in judgment of me, and telling the world I was not a decent person.

While I was still in the thick of this, I got into an argument with my father. He seemed to think that I should go ahead and give interviews to anyone who asked, so that I could get my frustrations off my chest and set the record straight. I didn't think that was a very good idea, and I knew I needed advice, so I began to look around for an attorney. I wanted the media to stop saying horrible things about me, and most of all I wanted them to stop showing those photographs.

I called a few lawyers in Fresno, but none of the people I spoke to inspired much confidence. I didn't know where to turn next. I had never needed a lawyer in my life and didn't even know what *type* of lawyer I needed.

The next day was February 10, my birthday, and Scott kept calling. I was very busy, and I didn't have time to talk, and he seemed like he had something on his mind. But for some reason he wouldn't get to the point. To compound matters, I had problems with the recorder, and I didn't manage to tape all of his calls. I called Buehler and told him and he said not to worry, no one expected perfection, and to do the best I could. This little glitch would come back to haunt me months later, however, when there was speculation in the media that I had neglected to tape all of our calls, or that I hadn't turned all of my tapes over to the police. Nothing could be further from the truth. I taped every call, some more successfully than others, and every single tape was hand-delivered to the authorities.

When Scott and I finally did connect, later that afternoon, he told me to go to Valley Children's Hospital and look for a certain streetlamp. There was a purple bush near the base of the lamp, and he had left something for me there. I went. How could I not go? I was curious. I found the streetlamp, and the bush, a lavender plant. Tucked deep inside the bush was a paper bag from Trader Joe's with several items in it. The first was a small silver box with the moon and sun on the lid; there was a silver and amber necklace inside. The bag also contained a copy of the Norah Jones CD, *Come Away with Me*, and a package of "Butterfly" wildflower mix. It was obvious that Scott had put a lot of thought into each choice.

There was a note in the bag: "These seeds as your life are soon to bloom. Bliss, joy, beauty will spring forth as warmth touches each. Your soil is not a stony place you have tilled good ground. You deserve wondrous ecstasy in all aspects of your life. All these things will be yours soon."

I felt badly for Scott. I remembered how defeated he had sounded in our last conversation, and I guess I was feeling slightly defeated myself. I sat in my car in the hospital parking lot with all my lovely gifts, and I cried.

That evening, my friend Denise threw a birthday party for me at her home. It was such a relief to be surrounded by friends that I kicked back and allowed myself to have a good time. In a matter of hours, I'd gone from sobbing in my car in a hospital parking lot to letting it all hang out with my closest friends. This is what my life had become.

I ended up spending the night at Denise's, and after she went to bed I turned on the news. I had not forgotten for a moment that my birthday coincided with Laci's due date, and I knew there had been a special vigil to commemorate it. The media was out in full force, of course. They had footage of the mourners listening to "I'm With You," a song by Avril Lavigne, and as I listened to the lyrics, I burst into tears:

> *I'm waiting in the dark*
> *I thought that you'd be here by now.*

When the segment ended, I turned off the television, dried my tears, and climbed into bed next to my sleeping daughter.

The next day I called Buehler to tell him about Scott's gifts. I also told him that I had an extra copy of *The Purpose-Driven Life*, an inspirational book by Rick Warren, and that I wanted to give one of my copies to Scott. The book is designed to help people understand and fulfill God's plan for them on earth, and I guess I still thought I could get through to Scott, even if everyone else had all but given up on him. "I want Scott to know God and to have hope through God and to try to learn something about being a good person," I told Buehler.

Buehler said he understood where I was coming from, and he told me he didn't see the harm in it. I sent the book to Scott's Modesto P.O. box, with a note explaining why I was sending him the book, and with one question: Did the Norah Jones CD—*Come Away with Me*—have any special meaning?

In the note, I asked him further to please sign the book, as a way of acknowledging that he intended to read it, and to write his thoughts in the margins as he made his way through the text. I reminded him that the book was supposed to be read a little at a time, and that he should try to get to it every day.

I also told him to destroy my note. I didn't want the media to find it.

* * *

On Valentine's Day, I went out with three girl-friends—none of us had dates—and I happened to see Paul and Lauren Benson making their way into a restaurant. It seemed as if they were getting on with their lives.

The next day, Scott called to thank me for the book. I was asleep when he called, and it took me by surprise. He asked me if I still had the note he'd written me, the one about the seeds of my life, and he asked me to read it to him. I went and got the note and read it to him, and he became very emotional and cried.

On February 18, police went to Scott's house with a warrant. According to the newspapers, the room he had discussed with Diane Sawyer, the room he'd cried over—"That door is closed until there's someone to put in there"—had been turned into a storage room. Police removed several bags of evidence from the home, and even impounded Scott's new truck.

The implications for Scott grew worse by the day. I realized I shouldn't keep talking to him, at least until the case was resolved, and—with Buehler's approval—I determined to tell him as much the next time he called. He called soon enough, of course, and I struggled to break the news to him without being hurtful. "Okay. Um . . ." I began, faltering. "I can't really say in light of current events, but um (sigh) I don't know really the right . . . right words to say but I'm just going to say it. . . ."

"Okay."

"However it comes out . . ."

"Yeah?"

"I think right now, for me, Scott, and really everything that has happened in the past fifty-plus days for myself and . . . and the family and you and everything that's going on right now . . . I think it would be best if you and I didn't talk anymore until there's resolution in this whole . . ."

"Yeah. I agree with that."

"Good. Good."

"You're right."

"Okay, well, that wasn't so hard."

"No, it's the right thing," he said.

"Huh?"

"It's the right thing so, yeah."

"Okay. So is there anything you want to say before, um, I say goodbye?"

"Yes, I mean, you know, I see the reason. Oh, well, and just be well."

"Likewise."

"Okay."

"Okay."

"I hope to talk to you in the future," Scott added.

"Okay, Scott."

"Good-bye for now."

217

"Huh?"

"Good-bye for now."

"Good life now?"

"Good-bye for now."

"Good-bye, Scott."

I set the phone down, half-expecting to feel relieved. But I didn't feel relieved. In cutting off my conversations with Scott, I got the feeling that I was cutting off my only link to Laci and her unborn child. Despite the odds, I wanted to believe that they were still alive. I knew I had done the right thing, though, and I gathered up the recorder and the tapes and turned them over to Buehler.

The next day, Thursday, February 20, an employee at American Body Works discovered that a Federal Express envelope had been left for me next door. It contained two books for Ayiana, *Happy Easter!* by Michelle Knudsen and *Corduroy's Easter* by Don Freeman. They were from Scott, and the package included a note: "For Amber's little one, Happy Birthday."

Scott called the next day to ask if I had received the book. I told him yes, and I thanked him, but I also asked him to please stop calling me. "If you have something to say, it might be better to use e-mail," I said. I gave him my e-mail address, and the next time I checked my computer there was a note from him. The return address immediately struck me: purposelife2003@yahoo.com.

In the days ahead, he wrote about the "four visions" he had for his life, but he didn't get specific, and from time to time he wondered about Ayiana. I wrote back that she was beginning to speak in complete sentences, and that I loved having conversations with her. "(T)hank you for sharing that with me," he replied. "It is a beautiful thing to be able, and be depended upon, to develop a wonderful little person." He went on to say that I was charged with developing her mind, and character, and soul to a great degree. He continued: "Have her follow in your footsteps and she will be great."

In a later e-mail, dated February 28, he expanded a little on his four visions, saying that one of them was "being able to spend time, at least 18 hours of every day, with my immediate family, by that I mean wife and child. I envision falling asleep in a hammock cradling the people I love. I see sailing on warm summer evenings and watching the stars appear." Another vision related to "a family continuing to grow together, challenging each other intellectually, growing as a loving unit, going beyond what individuals can get to by themselves."

He also said, "I strive to be positive in people's

lives, we all need to be. I will be." And he wrote about life with his family: "I got to fall asleep the other evening with my nephew on my chest, I was able to spend time with my youngest niece delivering Girl Scout cookies, and I was able to go to another nephew's class and tutor some children with math. These were the activities of last week and these are the things that matter, for these things I am going to target my life, to having positive strong relationships is the goal I keep in my head."

On March 5, the Modesto Police Department reclassified the Laci Peterson case: it went from a missing person investigation to a homicide. I called Buehler to try to get some information, but he wasn't really at liberty to talk about it. Still, it was clear that at this point everyone assumed Laci was no longer alive. I think I had known this was coming, and I was prepared for it. But that didn't make it any easier.

Scott called again, and I again asked him to please stop calling. I phoned Buehler and told him about the call and said I was concerned for my safety and for the safety of my daughter. He said he understood my anxiety, but that the police still had Scott under surveillance, and that he honestly didn't think I had anything to worry about.

A few days later, a friend phoned to tell me

she was going to Vero Beach, in Florida, and invited me to come along. For an entire week, I was almost a normal person. I took Ayiana swimming. We built sand castles together. We took long walks on the beach, looking for seashells. We wandered through shops. We ate in fun restaurants. I hardly thought about the case, or about Scott, for the entire time.

When I returned to Fresno, I found myself spending more and more time with Dave Markovich. Scott wasn't calling, but he was still sending e-mails. In one note, he told me he had just been out with his two nephews, flying a kite. In another, he said he had been helping rebuild a deck at a home for battered women when he noticed a man in his early twenties staring at him. He said he recognized the man as the young boy he had tutored years earlier at the St. Vincent de Paul Center for Homeless Children.

Dave wondered why I was still communicating with Scott. It didn't sit well with him. I pointed out that the communication was largely one-sided.

On April 13, the body of a full-term baby washed ashore in San Francisco Bay, near Richmond. The next day, police found the badly decomposed remains of a woman. Police

subsequently announced that they had posi-
tively identified the bodies of Laci Peterson, and
of her son, Conner.

I wept. I felt awful for Laci's family and
friends, all of those wonderful people who had
been so good to me that day in Modesto. As for
Scott, I didn't even want to think of the implications. But later, in a moment of weakness, I sent
him a one-line e-mail: "Were those the bodies of
Laci and Conner?"

Scott never replied.

It was the last time I ever communicated
with him.

On April 18, Scott was arrested at the Torrey
Pines Golf Course, in La Jolla. He had lightened
his hair to a reddish-blond, grown a goatee, and
he was carrying more than $10,000 in cash.
There were reports that he had been on his way
to Mexico.

But maybe not. Among the items police found
in Scott's car were a filet knife, a double-edged
dagger with a T-handle, a folding saw, duct tape,
and a shovel. There was also a map in his car,
which had been downloaded that very day. It
provided driving directions to my office.

Scott was returned to Modesto and booked
and pleaded not guilty to two counts of murder,
one for his wife, Laci, and one for his unborn
son, Conner.

Almost immediately, my phone started ringing. The reporters were back with a vengeance. One of the most persistent callers was one of Diane Sawyer's producers. She even stopped by American Body Works one day with a little gift—a velvet frog with a string of words stitched across the front: *How many frogs must I kiss before I find my prince*? It made me cry. There was also a little note. "This made me think of you. Hang in there."

The producer reached me on the phone later that same day, and she could see I was having a very rough time with all of this, so she suggested I call an attorney. She gave me the name of a woman in San Diego. I called her and was put through as soon as I identified myself. We spoke briefly about the on-going requests for interviews, and about what I might be able to do about the nude photographs and the fact that I never signed a release form, but I never followed up with her. San Diego seemed too far away.

When my father heard I was looking for an attorney, he did a little research on his own and came up with Gloria Allred's name. He reached her in Los Angeles, and they chatted briefly, and as soon as they got off the phone he called to tell me that she sounded great and that I should contact her. I had never heard of Gloria Allred, so I looked her up on the Internet. She had her own website. It said that she was a partner in the law firm of Allred, Maroko & Goldberg, in Los Angeles, and that she had been practicing law for more than twenty-seven years. The firm handled everything from discrimination to harassment, and Gloria had been singled out for her work on behalf of women's rights. I saw that she had represented the family of Nicole Brown Simpson during the O. J. Simpson trial, and that she'd had some involvement with Paula Jones's lawsuit against then-President Bill Clinton.

I called her and we spoke briefly, and she said she would be glad to fly up and meet me. I made arrangements with my church to meet her in a private room there, and we set a date. When I told Dave Markovich about her, he was less than supportive. "She's one of those feminists," he said.

"You don't know what you're talking about," I said. "Do you even know what a feminist is? It's not about male-bashing. I need someone who understands my situation and can handle the media. Besides, I don't even know if she's the one for me."

The following day, I received a letter from Scott. It had been sent from jail. "I am searching for ways to do service within these walls," he wrote. "I will find some way . . ."

And further along: "May 4th is Laci's birthday—she would have been 28—and I am asking close friends to fly a kite in her memory. She and Conner should not have been taken from the earth as they were. . . .

"My prayers are always that you and (the) little one are happy. I hope you can play together and laugh. You deserve the best in this world. Children are miracles that we get [to] watch and help with. What a gift." He signed it, simply, "Scott."

A few days later, I met Gloria at a private room at my church, the North Park Community Church, and the first thing that struck me about her was that she was smaller than I'd imagined. But she had a big, warm personality. We talked about my role in the case, and about what I might expect in the weeks and months ahead, and she said she was happy to represent me pro bono.

"Why?" I said.

"Well," she replied. "Why did you go to the police?"

"Because it was the right thing to do," I said.

"Well, that's why I want to represent you," she replied. "Because it's the right thing to do."

We spent two hours together. She asked me about my personal life, and shared some stories about her own life. I was amazed at how many common threads ran through our lives. By the time we were done, I felt completely connected to her, and I felt she was a very special human being.

Before she returned to the airport, I took her to meet my father, and he was very nervous around her. He knew much more about Gloria than I did, and he found her fame and reputation intimidating—but in a good way. I didn't know enough about her to be intimidated. When we parted ways, I told her I would think about everything we had discussed and pray and call her the next day.

I called early the next morning and made it official: I wanted her to represent me. She said she would draw up a contract and arrange a news conference as soon as possible. "It will help immensely if people see that you have representation," she said. "A lot of the harassment will stop right away."

On April 30, one of the networks interviewed Mark Geragos, an attorney, about the case. He was not involved, but he was a criminal lawyer, and he had strong opinions. He described Scott as "a cad" and noted: "When guys commit adultery, guys lie to a single woman in order to get them into bed." Two day later, Scott and his parents announced that they had hired Geragos to steer the defense.

On May 19, as the case continued to heat up, I flew to Los Angeles to meet with Gloria and one of her partners, Nathan Goldberg. She told me that Nathan would be handling some of the finer details, especially as we got closer to the trial, and that we would be holding a press conference that very day, right there in Los Angeles. Before I knew it, it was time to face the press. Gloria and I sat down and said a little prayer, and I remember that I got pretty choked up. She handed me a Kleenex. I was still clutching it when we went out to talk to the reporters.

"In addition to being a witness," Gloria said, "Amber is also a victim of Scott's deception. Victims are entitled to attorneys, as are witnesses . . .

"She has been offered money for interviews and she has refused and will continue to refuse those offers. We are committed to protecting the integrity of the prosecution, and we will not allow her testimony to be contaminated by offers of money for her story."

Gloria had told me that the defense would be quick to attack me, and she repeated this for reporters. "Whatever it is, we will be ready to defend Ms. Frey, for whom we have a great deal of respect. . . . It will be clear a thousand times over that she has been an innocent victim."

When the reporters tried to question me, I was as nervous as I'd been at that first news conference, and I replied as Gloria had instructed me to reply: "I don't think it's appropriate to talk about what might be contained in my testimony prior to my being called to the witness stand. Until that time I just want to lead a normal life and regain my privacy. I hope that everyone will understand and respect my wishes."

Then Gloria spoke again: "It is very difficult for a person who is a private figure to be thrust into the . . . international spotlight. Amber is a person of strong faith, she has strong family values and ties, and she doesn't wish to be a public figure."

Most of the reporters were attentive and respectful, but in the days ahead a few of them decided to focus on my "makeover" since the press conference in Modesto. I don't think they understood that that press conference had taken place under wildly different circumstances. I'd been holed up in a tiny massage room for most of the day, hiding from the press, and then I'd been rushed to Modesto by the police. I hadn't even had time to brush my hair properly, let alone put on a little makeup. Now that I looked slightly more put-together, everyone simply assumed I was beginning to enjoy my moment in the spotlight. Nothing could be further from the truth.

For a while, I just tried to get on with my life. It wasn't always easy. Part of the fallout from my relationship with Scott was the way it affected my friendships. It seemed that every day someone close to me would either abandon me or sell me out, from the woman at work who decided to share my story with a local radio reporter, to so-called confidantes who wanted to see their names in *People* magazine. I felt betrayed at every turn. Never had I needed people so much, and never had I felt so horribly isolated and alone.

On the other hand, Dave Markovich was really there for me, and we grew closer. In the weeks ahead, he proved to be a tremendous source of support.

Eventually, the press left me alone, realizing that I really had no intention of talking to them, and I enrolled in an esthetician school so that I could do facials as well as massages. I enjoy working as a massage therapist, but three or four massages in a row can be very hard on the body, and I was looking to mix things up a bit.

In August I moved my business again, to a lovely day spa in a charming community a few miles from Fresno. Everyone there was and has remained very supportive of me.

Whenever I was out in public—at the park with Ayiana, shopping for groceries, out to dinner—strangers recognized me, and they were invariably supportive. Many of them took the time to tell me that they were behind me

100 percent, and that they were proud of me for coming forward. Many simply said they were praying for me, which meant a great deal to me.

There were only two unpleasant encounters. One happened at esthetician school, where a woman asked if she could take my picture. I declined, politely, but she took my picture anyway. It was all I could do not to lose my temper and grab her camera.

Another time, I was having dinner with a friend, when a young woman at a neighboring table got rowdy and made some nasty comments about me. This was incredibly hurtful, but my friend urged me to ignore it. "Some people are going to see what they want to see," she said. "Even when the truth is staring them in the face, they can't recognize it."

The women were drinking a lot, and being belligerent, and they continued making nasty comments, and before long the manager escorted them to the door and asked them not to come back. He later came by the table to apologize to me, which I greatly appreciated.

Even Jon Buehler, who had been championing me from the beginning, didn't really have any idea how deeply the case was affecting my personal life. One time we were walking across a parking lot together and suddenly we were surrounded by a gaggle of women who began calling out: "Are you Amber Frey?! Are you Amber Frey?!"

Buehler was pretty amazed. He was rarely out in public with me, so he'd never seen this side of my upended life. "Man," he said when we were safely out of their clutches. "That was really something."

In September, I found out I was pregnant, and I broke the news to Dave. I had hoped he would be more understanding, but he said he wasn't ready for fatherhood. I told him that an abortion was not an option. I was very upset. But Dave was not thrilled about it, and he made that perfectly clear.

A few days later, I had lunch with my pastor's mother and told her about the pregnancy. I also told her about having had an abortion many years earlier, and that I had subsequently repented before God. She assured me that I was making the right decision. "We make love, but God makes babies," she said. "God has a plan for you. That child is meant to be here."

I felt better after that, though of course Dave remained upset. For a while, our relationship was on very rocky terrain. He told me the media would soon find out, and that before long I would become an object of ridicule.

"That's not the kind of support I was hoping for!" I said, bursting into tears. "And I don't care what anyone says. I have repented before God. This child is my responsibility and Ayiana's sibling. I'm not going to have an abortion. A human life is more important to me than my reputation."

In September, Gloria and I went up to Modesto and met with Dave Harris, the deputy district attorney for Stanislaus County, and Rick Distaso, the prosecutor. They didn't know whether I'd be called during the preliminary hearing, but they wanted to talk to me about the possibility. They advised me to listen carefully to all questions, to answer them as clearly and as concisely as possible, and to always answer honestly. And if I didn't know the answer to anything, I should simply say so. There was no shame in not knowing.

"There's nothing to it," Harris said.

I only wished I felt half as confident as he did.

For the next few months, my life was disrupted at every turn. I never knew until the last moment whether I was needed in Modesto, and I was always scrambling to make sure my mother could pick Ayiana up after school. Sometimes I'd be on the road, halfway to Modesto, and I'd get a call about yet another delay in the proceedings, prompted by yet another motion, and I would get off at the next exit and double back onto the freeway and return home.

In November, when the preliminary hearing finally got under way, I still didn't know whether I'd be called, but it didn't look at all likely. At this point, the defense team was well aware of my pregnancy, and I was told that Geragos was probably conflicted about how to handle it. He couldn't very well beat up on a pregnant woman, and the pregnancy might remind people of Laci's pregnancy, which would only make me that much more sympathetic.

I was never called.

On November 18, 2003, following an eleven-day preliminary hearing, Scott was ordered to stand trial for the murders of his wife and unborn child.

*"The day you went to the police,
you became Laci's voice."*

W hile the world waited for the Scott Peterson trial to get under way, I went back to work and to my esthetician classes. From time to time, a reporter would call, but I always declined to be interviewed, and they left me alone. For a while, anyway.

In December 2003, *The Enquirer* did a story about my pregnancy and before long everyone had jumped on the bandwagon. This was immensely upsetting, to both Dave and me, but we weathered the storm and got through it. Dave was still not happy about the impending birth, but he seemed to be coming to terms with it. I hoped things would be better by the time I delivered in the spring.

In March, jury selection got under way in the San Mateo County community of Redwood City, and once again the press began to call. Not directly, mind you. They called my parents, people at work, anyone who knew me, or *said* they knew me, and put the questions to them: *What does Amber think? How does Amber feel? Was Amber still in love with Scott?* I was surprised by the number of people out there who knew so much about everything I thought and felt. They seemed to know me better than I knew myself.

In March, also, I finished esthetician school, but my efforts to get things off the ground were derailed by all of the pretrial publicity. *The Enquirer*, up to its old tricks, said in a story that my pregnancy was going to prevent me from testifying.

"That's absolutely, 100 percent false," Gloria Allred told reporters. "Amber Frey will testify if she is subpoenaed to testify. . . . This is a tabloid report and it's ridiculous."

I was bothered by all of the renewed attention, and so was Dave. Some of the less considerate newspapers continued to refer to me as Scott Peterson's "mistress," notwithstanding the fact that I had been an unknowing, reluctant mistress, and Dave found this particularly irksome. I understood: I imagined it couldn't be easy to be reminded on an almost daily basis of my relationship with Scott, no matter how brief it had been—or the fact that it had been based on lies.

At around this time, I went to see my doctor to check on the course of my pregnancy. I was told that my baby was due on May 4. I didn't think much of this until I learned that May 4 was Laci's birthday. This was just too disturbing. A year earlier I had discovered that Laci's son, Conner, was due on February 10, *my* birthday, and now I had to deal with another unsettling coincidence. I asked my doctor if he would induce labor a week early.

On April 1, 2004, while I was preparing for the birth of my son, Sharon Rocha was in Washington, D.C., with President George W. Bush. In an elaborate Rose Garden ceremony, he signed the Unborn Victims of Violence Act, which makes it a crime to harm a fetus during an assault on a pregnant woman.

"As of today, the law of our nation will acknowledge the plain fact that crimes of violence against a pregnant woman often have two victims," Bush said. "The death of an innocent unborn child has too often been treated as a detail in one crime but not a crime in itself."

The law had taken five years to get through Congress, and it gained broad support following Laci's murder. It is also known as "Laci and Conner's Law."

On April 27, I gave birth to Justin Dean. He weighed exactly seven pounds, and he was gorgeous. Ayiana came in to meet her little brother, looking completely overjoyed, and I found myself weeping with happiness. I looked over at Dave, who seemed very happy himself. I hoped and prayed that we could put our relationship back on track.

By the time I got Justin home, the jury had been seated, and things were heating up. I tried not to think about the coming trial—I had a gurgling newborn to enjoy—but I was reminded of it at every turn. I'd be in my car and look up and see somebody in a neighboring car, smiling broadly and giving me a thumbs-up. Or I'd be shopping for diapers, and I'd be approached for my autograph. How was I expected to respond?

One day, at my bank, I heard a small voice call my name.

"Amber?"

I turned around. A young woman was studying me. She was very nervous, and her demeanor was almost apologetic. "You don't know me, and I'm sorry to bother you, and this might seem a little crazy to you . . ."

She trailed off. I could see she was having trouble talking to me, so I urged her to continue. "Yes?"

"Well," she stammered, "I, uh—I read in the paper that you're a Christian."

"That's right. I am."

"And—and I've been wanting to get hold of you but I didn't know how."

"What is it?" I asked.

"I had this dream. I was outside, in my street, jogging, and I saw Laci walking past. And Laci smiled and waved at me and said, 'Please tell my mother I'm okay.'"

It sent chills up my spine.

The young woman was crying by this time, and

I couldn't help myself—I started crying, too. She said that she felt God had been working through her to get this message to me. "After I had this dream, I prayed to God that I could somehow tell Laci's mother, and suddenly I run into you. Will you please let her know about the dream?"

I told her I would, and I gave her a hug and went on my way. I was still crying when I pulled out of the lot.

On June 1, the trial got under way in Redwood City. In his opening statement, Prosecutor Rick Distaso got right to the point. "Think back to 2002," he began. "Sharon Rocha was preparing for a Christmas Eve dinner. Laci and Scott were coming over at six. Sharon had put out the presents and set the table. At 5:15 p.m. the phone rings. It's the defendant, the son-in-law. 'Mom, is Laci there?' he asks. 'No,' Sharon answered. 'She's not supposed to be here until six.' 'I came home after a drive,' Peterson said. 'I went into the backyard, and the dog was there with the leash.' 'No, she's not here. All day. Did you call her friends?' 'No, I haven't,' Peterson replied. 'Call them, and call me back,' Sharon suggested. Peterson called again very quickly. 'I called back, and I'm not able to locate her. Laci's missing.' 'Did you check with the neighbors?' she asked. 'Laci might be delivering cookies.' 'No, I haven't,' he said. At that point, Sharon turned to her husband, Ron Grantski, and said: 'Something's wrong. Laci's missing.'"

Distaso also played an audiotape of my New Year's Eve telephone conversation with Scott, the one where he claimed to be in Europe, and where he talked lovingly about our future. I wondered whether those taped telephone conversations, and my relationship with Scott, were going to become one of the building blocks of the prosecution.

At the conclusion of his opening statement, Distaso said: "Ladies and gentlemen, this is a commonsense case. At the end of this case, I'm going to ask you to find the defendant guilty of the murder of Laci Peterson, as well as the murder of his son, Conner."

When it was Mark Geragos's turn to address the court, he said Scott was "stone cold innocent." He further said that Conner had been born alive, that there was evidence that his umbilical cord had been cut, and that Scott could not possibly have had anything to do with his death. "This is a murder case, and there has to be evidence in a murder case," he went on. But what did the police have? "Zip. Nothing. Nada. Not a thing!"

Geragos suggested that the police had failed to pursue evidence that would have led them to the real killer or killers; this created the expectation that he would turn up some likely suspects. As everyone now knows, this never happened, and it badly weakened his defense.

I had been advised by Gloria and Nathan not to follow the case, but there was really no getting away from it. Dave would mention something, or my dad would call to discuss it, and even clients felt compelled to share their thoughts and insights during their massages. And of course the headlines screamed at me from every corner newsstand.

On June 30, Shawn Sibley was put on the stand. When she was being cross-examined, she remembered that Scott had joked about putting the words "Horny Bastard" on his business card, but Geragos didn't treat it as a joke. She also said that Scott had told her he'd had a lot of one-night stands, and that he was tired of "bimbos"—which wasn't something she had fully shared with me. Unfortunately, Geragos didn't want to hear about the other Scott, the charming, well-mannered gentleman I met on November 20, 2002.

Shawn told the court that Scott had said he was single, and she talked about the day she discovered he might be married, noting that she called him and confronted him and that he had denied it. "If I find out you are lying, I'm going to kick the shit out of you," she said she told him.

She also said she'd been with me the night I discovered the truth about Scott, and about his missing wife, and that I had immediately called the police.

At one point, Geragos asked Shawn if she knew

where I'd been on December 24 and December 25, right around the time Laci was said to have disappeared. I think he was trying to suggest that I might have had something to do with the disappearance, and this didn't sit well with me at all.

I was equally disturbed by some of the comments my so-called friends were making to the press. They said I had been a party girl and had only begun settling down after the birth of my first child, Ayiana. They said I grew up "tough," the product of a broken home, and that I'd had a string of "unsavory boyfriends." And they were quick to remind the public—as if anyone needed reminding—about the nude photographs.

I have never pretended to be anyone other than who I am. And I have never pretended that my past has been free of mistakes. But it still hurt.

Gloria and Nathan had warned me about this. They had also warned me that the defense was going to be hard on me when they put me on the stand. It was standard operating procedure, they said. They knew it was painful, and they were going to help me get through it.

One of the valuable lessons I took away from this experience was a very simple one: you can't control what people say about you, but you *can* control how you respond to it. And I was getting better at it by the day. I was also helped by something a member of my church was kind enough to point out one Sunday. "Amber," she said, "the only difference between you and everybody else is that your life is on public display. We all have skeletons in our closets."

I knew my turn on the stand wasn't far off, but I honestly wasn't all that anxious about it. Even as a child, I had never been one of those kids who worried in advance about anything. If I had a big test coming up, it didn't hit me until I was sitting in class, with the test in front of me. And if I was going to Disneyland for the weekend, I didn't get overexcited until I walked through the gates.

In the weeks ahead, the proceedings slogged along. In late July, Geragos tried for the third time to declare a mistrial. I didn't honestly understand the finer points, or why he'd want to start again from scratch at a later date, and I could only conclude that—even at this early stage—he was already worried about losing.

On August 4, someone from the Stanislaus County Sheriff's Department was on the stand, talking about Shawn and Scott and how she had introduced us. People already knew this, of course, but I guess they wanted to cover it from every possible angle. The same witness also talked about the computers that had been confiscated from the Peterson home and noted that Scott had done some online research on fishing in San Francisco Bay.

The following week, it was my turn to appear,

and I was forced to get ready. I hadn't even thought about what I was going to wear, but I had recently given birth and none of my clothes fit properly. I went out to buy a few new outfits, and it was very stressful. I didn't know what people would read into my wardrobe. I didn't know how I was supposed to "act." In fact, the last thing I wanted to do was act. I just wanted to be myself, Amber Frey.

Nathan Goldberg came to the rescue. He said it was a courtroom, and the appropriate wardrobe would be quiet and conservative. He suggested skirts, and he told me to stay away from bright colors. "This is a serious case, and you should dress accordingly," he said. "Dress as if you were going to a shower or an afternoon tea." He could see I was confused: I'd never been to an afternoon tea in my life, and I'd recently been to a baby shower—in overalls. So Nathan tried to make it easy. "Amber, just get up there and be who you are," he said. "You can't do any better than that."

On August 9, we went up to Redwood City. Gloria and Nathan took me to the courthouse to give me a feel for the place. We walked around the deserted courtroom, and I even took a moment to sit in the witness chair. I said I felt pretty comfortable, but of course the room was empty.

We went back to the Marriott and checked in, and I experienced another of those disturbing coincidences. When Scott was arrested near Torrey Pines, police found a day planner on him. One entry was marked: *3-28—important date for Amber.* When investigators asked me about it, I told them that I really couldn't think of what the date might refer to, and that it didn't mean anything to me. But it meant something to me now: My room number at the Marriott was 328.

The following morning, which was to be my first day on the stand, both Gloria and Nathan came to get me. I heard a knock at my door and opened it, and for a moment I felt so dizzy that I almost passed out. I supported myself against the door, and they both looked a little concerned.

"Amber? You okay?" Gloria asked.

I nodded. "I guess I'm just a little nervous," I said.

"You look great," Nathan said. "I've never seen you look better."

I was wearing a basic black skirt suit and a pale gray top.

When we arrived at the courthouse, we were admitted through a side door, but as we approached I could see crowds of people milling about. Many of them shouted encouragement and support, waving or raising their fists high in the air. One man said, "God is with you, Amber! Stay strong!"

Before I was called to testify, I closed my eyes for a moment and said a little prayer. I knew I wasn't alone and that thousands of people were praying for me. I also felt strong. I felt I was there for Laci and Conner, and for women everywhere who had ever been victimized by violence. Then I heard someone call my name, and I stood and made my way down the narrow aisle. I could feel every set of eyes in the room on me, and I braced myself for what was to come. Here it was at last. I would be testifying against a man who had once talked to me about our beautiful future together. I knew he was sitting right there in that courtroom, probably staring at me at that very moment, but I refused to allow myself to look in his direction.

The court clerk asked me to state and spell my name, which I did, and Dave Harris was given permission to proceed with the direct examination.

"Miss Frey," he began, "I want to go back to around October, November of 2002. Did you know a person by the name of Shawn Sibley?"

"Yes."

I described Shawn as a best friend, and I said that she had met Scott and had thought we would be a good match. "And the person that you know as Scott Peterson," Harris asked, "do you see that person here in the courtroom today?"

"Yes."

"Could you point to that person and describe something he's wearing?"

I glanced over at Scott for a split-second, and

he was indeed staring at me. He looked gentle, almost puppyish, and I quickly looked back at Harris. "Blue, striped tie; gray suit."

The clerk of the court noted, "For the record, she has identified the defendant. Go ahead."

"I want to go back to that conversation with Shawn Sibley," Harris said, and before long we got into some painful territory, beginning with the first time I met Scott.

"Did you happen to notice if the defendant was wearing a wedding ring at the time?" Harris asked.

"No."

"Did he—so you did notice, or he didn't have a ring on?"

"He did not have a ring."

I was forced to admit that I spent that very first night with Scott, in his hotel room, and then I described seeing him again on Monday, and about going on a hike with him and Ayiana. I told the court about the Christmas tree, and I said Scott spent the night at my place and that we were intimate and talked afterward.

Harris wanted to know what we had talked about, and I told him about that, too: "I was talking about—I don't recall how the conversation was brought up, but about trust and how I felt about trust and lies and how it—for me and how I handled things. I—how—how it's easier—it's easier to handle truth, no matter what it is, versus a lie, and that knowing that a person could come to you with the truth is easier to handle than it later coming out that it was a lie. And basically just being truthful and how I responded to that."

"Did the defendant make any comments or agree or disagree during that part of the conversation?"

"Yes."

"What did he say?"

"He complimented me on my way of thinking about other people or how to handle situations that we were talking about."

Later, Harris asked me about the day I discovered the truth—or, more precisely, what I *thought* to be the truth: "He said he had lied to me about ever being married, and he had stated that sometimes for himself, when people would ask, it was easier for him to say that he was not or never had been married. . . ."

"Did he tell you why he had lied about being married?"

"That it was painful for him."

"Did you ask him, or did he explain why it was painful for him to say he had been married?"

"Yes."

"What did the defendant tell you?"

"That he had lost his wife. . . ."

The whole experience was very trying, emotionally. For most people, it was just a story, but to me it was part of my life, a very painful part. I tried not to look at the individual faces because I was afraid that even a small expression of sympathy might reduce me to tears, and I tried not to look at the faces of the jurors because they seemed riveted, and their interest made me doubly aware of how much was at stake.

"Now let's kind of break this up into little pieces," Harris was saying. "When you—when the defendant comes to you on December 9, and tells you this about losing his wife, that he had lost his wife, did you have any idea that he was doing this because of the conversation he had with Shawn Sibley?"

"No."

Later, he asked me about the fateful night when Richard Byrd reached me at the Bensons, confirming my worst fears about Scott.

"Before Richard Byrd had passed that information on to you, did you know the defendant was married?"

"No."

"Did you know that he had a wife by the name of Laci?"

"No."

"Did you know that his wife was missing?"

"No."

Later, when Harris played some of the tapes, I could barely listen. I hung my head, and I was forced to sit there and relive all of the painful lies.

* * *

At the end of my first day of testimony, Gloria faced the press. "I'm very pleased on how Amber is doing," she said. "I'm very proud of her. It's a very stressful situation. I don't know anyone who would want to trade places with Amber Frey and be a witness in a high-profile murder case. . . . I think what we saw this morning from her testimony are the number of lies—and we're just on the very first morning—that Scott Peterson told to her. . . ."

In a later interview, with CNN reporter Heidi Collins, she said, "(W)hat kind of husband calls from the vigil that is being set up for his missing pregnant wife and is on the phone with his woman friend, Amber, and has this ebullient, man about town, bon vivant conversation with her, lighthearted, on New Year's Eve, where he's saying to her, 'I miss you,' and 'Hi, sweetheart.' And 'I'm at the Eiffel Tower,' and 'I'm in Paris.' Now, does that sound like a grieving husband who's missing his pregnant wife? I don't think so. And I think it was totally inappropriate, and I think the jury could find from that, that perhaps he wasn't a grieving husband at all."

When Collins asked Gloria if I was nervous, which I think was obvious to anyone who was watching, she was very kind. "She was a little bit nervous," she said. "That would be natural in such a high-pressure situation. She did very,

very well. She was very specific, Heidi, in her recollection of events. She gave great detail. And, of course, she was so important because she did agree to assist law enforcement by tape-recording those telephone calls with Scott Peterson after Laci disappeared."

At the end of the day, we returned to the Marriott. Dave and his parents had come up to stay with me and help with the baby. I was breast-feeding Justin at the time, and throughout the day I had taken advantage of every little break to nurse him. He was always ravenous, and I invariably returned to the witness box more exhausted than ever.

That first night, I was so tired I could barely eat. I looked at Dave's mother, who is a beautiful Christian woman, and I said, "This has all been inevitable, from the moment I met Scott Peterson. But whatever else has happened, the one thing I am supremely thankful for is that little Justin is here with me today."

"Me, too," she said, and we hugged each other.

I really appreciated having Dave and his family in Redwood City with me. During the day they sat in a little room near the courtroom, caring for Justin and waiting for me to show up on my break. Everyone knew about little Justin, even Judge Alfred Delucchi. From time to time, just before the break, the judge would lean close to me and say, "Amber, don't rush things with the baby. Take all the time you need."

I remained on the stand for several days, and I was stared at everywhere I went. I thought, *If this is what it means to be a celebrity, it's overrated.* And every day the court heard Scott's recorded voice over a set of loudspeakers. They heard him make all sorts of promises, every last one of them based on lies. They even heard him talk about popular culture: "Ooh! The best movie ever made is *The Shining.*"

After that session, Gloria told reporters: "It's a film about a husband whose mental health is deteriorating significantly and as a result he has to attempt to kill his wife."

When I heard myself, on tape, telling Scott that "robbers don't steal people," I felt a little ripple of smug amusement in the courtroom, and sensed an almost palpable shift in the tone of the trial. I believe more and more people were becoming convinced that Scott Peterson was not the innocent man he pretended to be.

I was sitting in the gallery at this point—it was too much, emotionally speaking, to listen to these recordings from the witness box, as if I were on display—and from time to time Gloria put her arm around my shoulders to comfort me.

Then they played a clip that made me break down and sob:

"I did everything possible to protect my baby

and me!" I heard myself saying, my voice cracking with emotion. "I told you this. I worked forty-plus hours a week—because I wasn't going to ask for any help from anyone. And I did this on my own. I went to school. I had my baby, I did this all with her. I didn't need this in my life. I didn't need for someone to come in and to fuck all of it up."

"I know that, Amber," Scott replied.

"You weren't supposed to be someone that would bring me down!"

"No, I don't want to be."

"You were supposed to be someone to be there for me!"

Later, during a break, I told Nathan that I was finding the experience painful *and* embarrassing. "Never for a moment did I imagine they were going to play these tapes in court," I said. "I guess I wasn't thinking that far ahead. And now everyone in the world can listen to them; everyone can see me being humiliated."

"Not at all," he said. "Everyone can see you standing up for yourself, and standing up for Laci Peterson."

"That's exactly right," Gloria agreed. "The day you went to the police, you became Laci's voice. All this time, you've been speaking for Laci."

The court also listened to a portion of my February 19 conversation with Scott:

"I think right now, for me, Scott, and really everything that has happened in the past fifty-plus days for myself and . . . and the family and you and everything that's going on right now . . . I think it would be best if you and I didn't talk anymore until there's resolution in this whole . . ."

"Yeah. I agree with that."

"Good. Good."

"You're right."

The conversation ended with three little words: "Goodbye for now."

The following Monday, when they again played the tapes, I was allowed to return to the gallery. I remember I was wearing a fitted gray suit, very conservative, and that I had a copy of the transcripts in my lap. I followed along, not looking up at anyone, and this went on for several days.

"I'm saying now, was Laci aware of the situation about me?"

"Yes."

"She was?"

"Yeah."

"Really? How did she respond about it?"

"Fine."

"Fine?"

"Yeah."

"An eight-month pregnant woman fine about another woman?!"

"You don't know all the facts, Amber. You don't know all the facts. . . ."

They also played one of our very last conversations, when I had sensed, mistakenly, that Scott might be on the verge of confessing:

"You know all the answers to the things you want to know," Scott said.

"I do?"

"Yes."

"I do?"

"Yes."

"How do I know?"

"I wish I could tell you, but you've guessed the answers to all of them."

"How do I have the answers, Scott?"

"Well, you don't have the answers, but you've guessed at them and you know them and it's just going to take time and trust for me to—not trust—but time for me to be able to tell you."

When I was done with the direct examination, the newspapers were buzzing: they felt my testimony had been very damaging to Scott. It went beyond the fact that he was a world-class liar. Here was a man whose pregnant wife was missing, and yet—in his conversations with me—he seemed totally unaffected by it; he was a man without a care in the world.

Before long, however, it was time for the cross-examination, and suddenly I was on trial. Geragos tried to portray me as a woman who was desperate for a relationship, and who had had plenty of evidence that Scott was married—but that I chose to ignore the evidence because I didn't want to see it. He tried to shame me about that first night in Scott's hotel room, and he attempted to describe my relationship with Scott as a fling that had been fueled by need and sex and alcohol.

I was ready for him, however; my attorneys had prepared me. They had told me that the defense was going to make every effort to put my entire life in an unflattering light.

I also had God on my side.

Early on, Geragos told the court that on December 26, I called Scott fourteen times. And he was right, I did: I wanted to thank him for his Christmas gift. It had nothing to do with obsession. Quite the contrary, by that time I was already beginning to have misgivings about Scott.

"Did he ever physically hurt you?" Geragos asked.

"No."

"He never told you that he loved you, right?"

"Not in those words," I said.

He then played one of our taped calls, the one in which I said, "I assume . . . possibly that she's missing because you love me, right?"

That was a tough moment. I would have never asked that question, but I'd been prodded to do so by police. This had occurred during one of their "coaching sessions," up in Modesto, at the precinct.

"Amber, she's missing because someone abducted her," Scott replied.

"Somebody abducted her?"

"That's what we think happened."

"Really?"

"Yeah. She would not run off."

"Okay."

"Someone took her."

At the end of each day, my attorneys and I would take an escalator to a rear entrance, and exit through a side door, avoiding reporters. And when we got back to the hotel, I'd go to my room and rest with Justin while Dave's mother made me something to eat.

Later, I'd meet with Gloria and Nathan, and we'd review my day on the stand. "If I had to grade you," Nathan said a couple of times, "I'd give you an A-minus." Then he would remind me to raise my voice a little, that it was sometimes hard to hear me. And he showed me how I might try to paint a clearer picture of a certain situation if I felt that Geragos was attempting to cut me off. "You could say, 'Can I explain that further, Your Honor?,' and you might get a chance to clarify things for the jurors."

It was hard to keep track of everything that was expected of me, but the hardest part was the way I was being forced to relive those many painful moments. Every time a reference was made to something that had happened between Scott and me, and every time I heard our voices on tape, it hurt. I was being taken back in time to each conversation, and my emotions were all over the place.

It was exhausting, and very painful, but I wasn't the only one in pain. On more than one occasion, Laci's mother and stepfather left the room, unable to listen. My heart went out to them.

Once, while I was breastfeeding Justin, Laci's mother came into the room. We smiled at each other and she again thanked me for my courage. Suddenly I remembered the nervous young woman I'd met at the bank, the one who had had a dream about Laci, and I very much wanted to share it with Mrs. Rocha. But I was afraid of causing her more pain. This was made worse by the fact that I was sitting there with my infant son, which could only have reminded her of her terrible loss, of the grandson she never met. A moment later she waved and smiled her sad smile and left the room.

Back in court, Geragos asked whether I had always fully cooperated with police. "Did you ever not turn over tapes?" he wondered.

"I turned over every tape that I recorded," I said.

"Did you ever make or receive calls from Scott Peterson that you didn't immediately tell detectives about?" he asked.

"No," I said.

"At any point did you hide any information . . . from the Modesto Police Department?" he prodded.

"No."

Then he asked me whether I had offered to lie for the police: "(Did) you tell them you could basically use the ruse that you were pregnant and they could use that . . . and see if that would elicit some information?"

"That was the concept," I admitted. "At that point, I was willing or open to anything . . . in assisting the police, if that would help in any way."

"The idea was to try to get him to admit something, to admit some involvement—that he had something to do with Laci's disappearance?" he asked.

"I questioned him many times in different ways, yes."

It was true. The ruse had been my idea. My period had been late, and I thought it might shake Scott up, but Buehler didn't much like the idea. He thought Scott was dangerous and unpredictable, and he didn't want to put me at risk.

After that day's testimony, Gloria once again came to my defense. "I think that a lot of the arguments that Geragos engaged in were just total garbage," she said. "For example, yesterday Geragos tried to demean the relationship between Amber and Scott, by implying that it was all about sex. However, you can examine the more than twenty hours of tape-recorded conversations, with more than 142 recorded calls, and you will not hear any discussion of sex on those tape-recorded conversations."

Some nights, back in the hotel room, I would watch parts of the coverage on the news. I would hear what the various reporters had to say, and I found myself thinking about what I had done wrong, or how I could have done better—not only on the stand, but with my life. These thoughts often kept me up at night at a time when I desperately needed sleep.

It was hard for Dave, too. I never lost sight of the fact that once again he was being forced to contend with my past. Jealousy is a strange beast, and retroactive jealousy is stranger still, but logic doesn't make it go away.

As my testimony began to wind down, I tried to come to terms with the enormity of what lay ahead. I kept hearing about myself on television, and reading about myself in the papers, and people continued to say that my testimony had been incredibly damaging to the defense. I began to wonder what would happen if Scott was found guilty, and—even more troubling—if he was sentenced to death.

I talked to Gloria and to Nathan and to Buehler. It was scary. After all, whatever else one might say about Scott Peterson, he was a human being. He had a family. I had seen his par-

WITNESS

ents. I had seen his siblings. I had seen his mother cry.

"You are just part of the larger puzzle," Gloria explained. "If he is found guilty, he is found guilty as a result of everything that was presented in court. And he is found guilty by the jury, not by any individual."

Gloria assured me that I was doing the right thing, and as if to prove her point she brought copies of the hundreds of e-mails that were pouring into her office by the day.

> "You have touched the hearts of many people and we are all praying for you!"
>
> "Please tell Amber she represents millions of us women."
>
> "Let Amber Frey know that thousands of people are behind her, sending her strength and best wishes in the difficult days ahead."
>
> "Her sincerity really shines through."
>
> "I want you to know how much your courage has done for me."
>
> "Ms. Frey, by your actions . . . you have a wonderful legacy to pass on to your children: courage, strength, truth, and the importance of standing up for justice."
>
> "Amber, as well as Laci, is just another sweet girl who hoped for love and understanding. We should all be able to dream

that dream without fear of being victimized or murdered."

"I hope Amber can find a partner someday who is worthy of her love and affection."

"Stay strong, Amber! You are in this situation through no fault of your own, and there are legions of people out here who recognize and know this."

"Please tell Amber I think she's a hero."

"I don't think very many young women her age would have had the courage to go to the police . . . and then agreed to record the conversations. . . . Without her brave actions, it's entirely possible that Scott Peterson would be acquitted of these terrible murders. As good an attorney as Mark Geragos is, it's going to be very difficult for him to undo the impact of the tapes."

I wept when I read these. And I wept when Buehler took me aside to tell me that his own daughter had described me as a hero. "She said you were her new role model," he noted. "You are everyone's sister, daughter, friend. You should be very proud of yourself."

I also wept when Detective Craig Grogan came by to congratulate me. "You were great," he said.

"I don't know," I replied uncertainly, and I

guess I lowered my face. "Sitting there, listening to myself on tape—I felt completely humiliated."

Grogan reached over and gently lifted my chin with the tips of his fingers. "Hold your head high, Amber. You've earned it."

Coming from Detective Grogan—a warm teddy bear of a man—this only made me cry harder.

I went home at the end of August, and the trial dragged on. I tried not to pay much attention to it, but it was everywhere, and virtually unavoidable. I also heard rumors—the same rumors everyone else heard: That Scott had bought several phony college diplomas less than a week before Laci disappeared. That people close to him had advised him to deny everything. That there had been many other "mistresses" before me. That police had found pornography on his computer. That he had hired a prison gang to kidnap and kill his wife.

Reporters tried to reach me from time to time, but of course I was under a gag order and not permitted to discuss anything with anyone. Gloria spoke on my behalf: "I can only make a general statement that when [the police] felt it was appropriate to seek her assistance, she assisted whenever and wherever she could. She has fully cooperated and made many personal sacrifices in order to assist law enforcement."

On September 8, a DNA expert testified that a

hair found in Scott's boat was "consistent with" Laci's.

On September 21, the jury was permitted to watch the interviews Scott gave to Gloria Gomez and Diane Sawyer shortly after Laci's disappearance. In a strange way, you could say that both news reporters ended up testifying for the prosecution.

Later in the month, Detective Craig Grogan took the stand and said the police had "forty-one reasons" to search San Francisco Bay for Laci and Conner: Scott's alibi had changed. He had told no one about the purchase of the fishing boat. A search dog had picked up Laci's scent at the Berkeley Marina. Scott was using the wrong kind of fishing tackle. Scott had whistled with evident relief when he was told that police had found an anchor in the Bay, not the body they'd been expecting. (He didn't know his line had been tapped.) A boat cover that had been in the back of Scott's truck later turned up in a shed at his house. The list went on and on.

Scott had told investigators that he had been fishing in San Francisco Bay on the day of Laci's disappearance, and—months later—her body turned up not far from the marina where he had launched his boat. The fact that Scott had placed himself in the area where both bodies were recovered turned out to be among the most damaging evidence against him. There was also the

issue of the missing cement. Around the time of
Laci's disappearance, Scott had reportedly gone
to Home Depot and purchased more than fifty
pounds of cement mix. He told investigators
that he had used it to make an anchor for his
new boat, which was much cheaper than buying
one, but he couldn't account for the bulk of it. Investigators suspected he had used it to weigh
down Laci's body.

On October 8, I went to a church retreat in Wonder Valley, about an hour's drive from Fresno.
The principal speaker talked about "women of
influence" and about the fact that each one of us
had a God-given purpose in life. It was a two-
night retreat, and on the second night the
speaker talked about Sara, from the Bible. She
said Sara was a fallen woman, but that God had
turned her into a woman of influence.

She put it in a way that made me relate to
Sara. Sara's life had been open to public
scrutiny, and it was clear that she had not always made the right choices, but she had found
her way back.

My life had been similarly exposed, and I had
felt pain and the judgment of others. But I took
solace from the fact that God had used Sara as
an example to others, and I hoped He would use
me in the same way.

Before I left the retreat, I took a moment to

thank the speaker. "Amber," she replied, "God will use you. *If you let him.*"

I left the retreat feeling replenished and full of optimism. I had my whole future before me, and—more important—I had *today*. The Bible says, "Tomorrow never comes." I was determined to make use of every day. And if God wanted to use me, in His own time and way, I was ready.

I had dinner with Gloria a few nights later. She had brought along another stack of e-mails, and I was struck by one in particular. The woman had written, "Laci's life has been taken, but Amber's life has been saved."

I looked over at Gloria, who had become such an important part of my life during this terrible ordeal, and whom I had come to know in a deeply personal way. And knowing what I knew about Gloria, knowing everything she had endured in her own life, I was filled with renewed hope.

The Biblical Sara had made mistakes, but at the end of day God had used her as an example and had used her to influence people in a positive way. Looking back on my own mistakes, I thought I could make a difference in people's lives, too. Sitting there that night with Gloria, thinking ahead, thinking about the future, I was overcome by a sense of power and possibility. I didn't know what lay ahead, but I knew I was on the right path, and I felt incredibly good about myself.

I started crying, and Gloria did her best to comfort me. "No, no," I said, wiping away the tears. "I'm happy! I can't remember the last time I was this happy."

I finally understood that everything that happens in one's life happens for a reason. I felt I was finally finding my way. And I felt that God had big things in store for me. "I don't know what they are," I told Gloria, "but I know a lot of good things lie ahead."

On October 26, Scott's parents took the stand. They denied that Scott had ever been trying to flee the country and said that the large amount of cash in his possession was connected to the recent purchase of a vehicle.

Jacqueline Peterson walked to the witness stand with her oxygen tank—she suffered from chronic bronchitis—and Geragos waited until she was comfortably seated. "You are Scott Peterson's mother, right?" he asked.

"Proudly so, yes," she answered.

This made me indescribably sad. Whatever Scott had done—and nothing had been determined at this point—he had once been her little boy. I have two children of my own. I'm not sure there's anything in the world that compares to the love of a parent for a child.

269

When Mrs. Peterson was cross-examined by Distaso, the story didn't hold up very well. She said she couldn't remember every detail, especially those pertaining to the money. "It was such a terrible time," she explained.

Scott's father, Lee, was reminded of the day that Scott was arrested and said he had invited his sons to Torrey Pines. "I was going to get three of my boys together to play golf, to have a little normalcy in our life," he said. But it was not to be. Scott reached one of his brothers on his cell phone to say he was being tailed by private investigators. "The last thing I need is a picture of me playing golf to show up in the media," he noted.

Neither Scott nor the family knew who had been tailing Scott—they assumed it was probably another tabloid reporter—and only later did they discover the truth: The police were closing in on him. A few days earlier, the bodies of his late wife and his unborn child had been recovered in San Francisco Bay, and they felt they had enough evidence to arrest him.

After twenty-three weeks of testimony and 184 witnesses, it was time for the closing arguments. "He wants to live the rich, successful, freewheeling bachelor life," Rick Distaso told the jurors. "He can't do that when he's paying child support, alimony, and everything else. . . . He didn't want to be tied to this kid the rest of his life. He didn't want to be tied to Laci for the rest of his life. So he killed her."

Distaso said Scott's two lives were finally catching up with him, and that there was only one possible conclusion: "(T)his man is guilty of murder."

When it was Geragos's turn, he pointed at Scott and plunged right in: "Do you all hate him?" he asked. "That's the sum total of what we heard yesterday. Four hours about [how] he's the biggest jerk to walk the face of the earth, he's the biggest liar to walk the face of the earth. You should hate him, you should hate him, you should hate him. Don't bother with the five months' worth of evidence."

He was being ironic, of course. He told jurors that they couldn't convict a man simply because they didn't like him; that they had to convict on the basis of the evidence.

The next few days were very confusing. Two members of the jury were replaced on two consecutive days, including the jury foreman, and no one expected a quick verdict.

On Friday, I took Ayiana to school and went to have breakfast with a girlfriend. I had Justin with me. In the middle of breakfast, my cell phone rang. It was Gloria. "Amber," she said, "they're going to have a verdict at one o'clock."

I was stunned.

*"I can do everything through Him
who gives me strength."*

I picked Justin up and left breakfast and rushed home, trying to stay calm. I felt strangely anxious and teary-eyed. I kept thinking, *This is it. This is really it.* But I didn't know what to expect. I didn't think a not guilty verdict was even a remote possibility. A more likely scenario was that the jurors were hopelessly dead-locked, and that they were going to announce that they couldn't come to an agreement. But could that still happen at this point? What was it Gloria had said? *They're going to have a verdict at one o'clock.*

I had made arrangements to watch the verdict at a friend's house, where no one could find me, so I grabbed Justin and raced home to get a few things. Ayiana was still in school, so I didn't have to worry about her for a few hours, and I thought it might be best to have my mother pick her up. Today of all days, I didn't want to deal with the press.

My cell phone was ringing when I walked into the apartment, it rang the whole time I was there, and it continued to ring as I returned to my car. I ignored it.

As I pulled away, with Justin tightly strapped into his car seat, I saw a news van coming down the street. I knew it would be the first of many. I kept checking my rearview mirror to make sure no one was following me.

My friend was at work, and when I arrived at her house I let myself in and set Justin on a blanket on the floor and turned on Court TV. The experts were weighing in with their opinions. Guilty. Not guilty. First degree. Second degree.

I was trying to stay calm. My cell phone rang, and I jumped. I saw from the caller ID that it was Dave. He had gone to the apartment to watch the verdict, and he told me there were reporters outside.

"I know," I said. "I was just there."

"You okay?" he asked.

"Sort of," I said, though I wasn't; not really.

Shortly after one o'clock, the jurors filed into court. There were no cameras in the courtroom, but the place had been wired for sound, and dozens of news crews and reporters were parked outside, waiting for the decision. Hundreds and hundreds of people had shown up to hear the news as it happened.

When the verdict was read—"Guilty!"—a huge cheer went up from the crowd.

I was already crying. I didn't know what I felt exactly, but I do know that I was completely overwhelmed. For two years, Scott Peterson had taken over my life, and it was finally over. The pain. The heartache. The lies. The personal attacks. The ridicule. The way complete strangers had had the gall to question my integrity and my morals.

But no more. That would all end now.

I kept the TV on, but I muted the sound, and I thought back to a recent conversation with Gloria Allred. I told her that I felt tremendous empathy for the jurors. "There's such pressure on them to do the right thing," I said. "And, at the end of the day, what is the right thing?"

"The right thing is to weigh the evidence against Scott," she replied.

I had often prayed for the jurors. I had asked God to give them the strength to find their way, but also to help them stand firm in their beliefs.

From the jubilant response outside the courtroom, it was clear that the vast majority of the country was very pleased with the verdict. I can't say I was cheering, but I was definitely relieved. The trial was over. We had a verdict. Justice had been served.

More e-mails poured into Gloria's office:

> "All I can say is if not for your client Amber, that low-life would have escaped with his terrible crime."
>
> "Just wanted to say how admirable Amber Frey is and to say Thank You! for her

willingness to stand up and tell the truth about Scott Peterson."

"I would appreciate it if you would let Ms. Amber Frey know that there are many who appreciate her for doing the right thing. She has a great deal of integrity, decency, honesty and faith. If she hadn't been willing to go to the police, the investigation could not have gone as it did."

"I would be so grateful if you could just tell her how thankful I am for her courage and honesty in coming forward, and for everything she did to bring justice to Laci and Conner and closure to Laci's family. It took a lot of guts to do what she did."

"She has proven to be the kind of human being we should all strive to be. . . . You've made your mark on the world, Amber!"

I don't know if I've made my mark on the world, but I'm young, and I have my whole life ahead of me—and I intend to do my best.

Scott had already left his mark on the world, a very dark mark indeed, and there was no undoing it. The verdict may have provided closure for Laci's family, but it couldn't bring Laci back. For the Petersons, the future seemed equally troubling, and doubtless just as painful. The son and brother they loved had been convicted of a double murder. He had taken two lives and, one way or another, he was going to pay with his own.

On November 30, 2004, just a few days after Thanksgiving, the penalty phase got under way. The jurors were being asked to decide whether Scott would spend the rest of his life in prison, without the possibility of parole, or face death.

The media waited breathlessly for the results, and legal experts were quick to volunteer their opinions. Several of them seemed to think that Scott would be better off with a death sentence, since it would be many years—if ever—before the sentence was carried out. I was surprised to learn that only ten prisoners had been put to death in California since 1978, when the state reinstituted capital punishment. As one lawyer pointed out, death-row inmates had their own cells, and this kept them relatively safe. If Scott was relegated to the general prison population, there was a good chance he wouldn't survive.

Two years earlier—almost to the day—I had met Scott at the Elephant Bar, and in the heady weeks that followed I had come to believe that we were moving in the right direction. We were moving quickly, certainly, perhaps *too* quickly, and I had some misgivings early on, but I had really liked this man, and I had allowed myself to imagine a future with him at my side.

Now, for all intents and purposes, his life was over. All that was left was the jury's decision: the penalty phase. Would he get life in prison, or would he be sentenced to death?

"How do you feel about the verdict, Amber?"

I heard that question a great deal in the days following the verdict. How did I feel? I felt humbled. I felt justice had been served.

"Do you think Scott Peterson should be put to death?"

I heard that a great deal, too, and I have to admit that I didn't have an answer. I wasn't sure how I felt about the death penalty, and I'm still not sure. Some people think it's barbaric. Others believe the punishment should fit the crime, and they even cite scripture to support their arguments. If you take a life, they say, you should pay with your life.

But the Bible also teaches us to turn the other cheek. Matthew 5:38: "You have heard that it was said, 'An eye for an eye and a tooth for a tooth.' But I say to you, Do not resist one who is evil. But if any one strikes you on the right cheek, turn to him the other also; and if any one would sue you and take your coat, let him have your cloak as well; and if any one forces you to go one mile, go with him two miles. Give to him who begs from you, and do not refuse him who would borrow from you. You have heard that it was said, 'You shall love your neighbor and hate your enemy.' But I say to you, Love your enemies and pray for those who persecute you, so that you may be sons of your Father who is in heaven; for He makes His sun rise on the evil and on the good, and sends rain on the just and on the unjust."

As I was trying to make sense of all of this, I received a beautiful, leather-bound copy of *The Purpose-Driven Life*, a gift from Rick Warren, the author, with my name embossed on it in gold. In his inscription, he said he had been praying for me. I was familiar with the book, of course, I had even given Scott a copy, and I was deeply moved by the gift. I once again found myself comforted by Mr. Warren's wise words.

One night, while I was rereading the book, Nathan called to check up on me. "Have you forgiven Scott?" he asked.

"I forgave him a long time ago," I said.

"I'm surprised," he said.

"I don't think I had a choice," I replied. "Until I forgave Scott, I felt I couldn't move forward. I felt I wasn't free to get on with my life."

Once, long ago, Scott Peterson had charmed me. He was good at that. He knew how to charm people. He even knew how to make them fall in love with him. But there was nothing on the inside. He was an empty vessel.

To me, Scott Peterson would always be a wolf in sheep's clothing.

There was only one thing left for Scott to do and that was to seek forgiveness from God. He was beyond earthly salvation, but he could still repent, and he could still be redeemed.

I prayed for Scott, and I prayed for his family. And I prayed for Laci's family, and for her friends, and for all those wonderful people who reached out to me during those dark early days after Laci's disappearance.

Some of those same people took the stand during the penalty phase of the trial, and I found myself praying for them, too. Laci's mother, Sharon Rocha, recalled her first Mother's Day without Laci, "I laid on the floor and cried most of the day because she should have been there and should have been a mother also. That was taken away from her.

"She gave me a picture of the sonogram. It's the only picture I have of the baby, and it was taken on December 14. The next day, December 15, was the last day I saw her. . . .

"I miss her," she told the court. "I want to know my grandson. I want Laci to be a mother. I want to hear her called 'Mom.'"

She seemed to be speaking of this as if it were still a possibility, and I found myself fighting tears.

Laci's stepfather, Ron Grantski, also took the stand. He said Laci was trusting almost to a fault. "I grew up in big cities and was taught to be on my guard and watch out. Laci was never on guard; never watched out."

Laci's younger sister, Amy, also took a turn. "It was the worst thing you could think about, like a nightmare," she said. And Laci's older brother, Brent, testified as well: "I miss her very much. I try to remember the good memories we have of each other, but they're overshadowed all the time by how she died . . . and maybe her knowing who did it. I don't think I've ever heard her be more excited than the day she called me up to tell me she was pregnant. She was going to be a great mother."

On Thursday, December 2, Scott's family told their side of the story. "He was sunny, motivated, always took care of business, always had a direction," Lee Peterson said of his son. "I love him very much. I have great respect for him and all these wonderful memories about him as a little guy growing up. . . . He woke up smiling and went to bed smiling."

How could I not be moved to tears by that, too? For a moment, you could almost forget what Scott had done. But only for a moment.

I imagine Laci's family will never forget, not even for a moment. There will always be a huge hole in Sharon Rocha's heart.

And it's unlikely that Scott's family will ever forget. They will be forever haunted by the difference between the son they thought they knew and the one who did those horrible things that no one ever suspected he was capable of doing.

One family wants to see him put to death, and I can understand this. The other wants his life spared, and I can understand this, too.

I wonder which option Scott would choose? Would he be better off living out the rest of his days behind bars, thinking about what he had done to his wife and unborn son? Or would he choose to end it?

In his shoes, what would any of us do?

There are times when God does indeed work in mysterious ways. And when we're in the thick of it, when we feel ourselves being brought low by the struggle, we seldom understand why these terrible things have befallen us, or why we are being tested. But in time the struggles make us stronger.

Philippians 4:13: "I can do everything through Him who gives me strength."

Scott was doubtless struggling, too, and he's struggling still, and he needs strength, too—the strength to seek forgiveness. It's there if he looks for it:

Luke 15:1–7: "What man of you, having an hundred sheep, if he lose one of them, doth not leave the ninety and nine, in the wilderness, and go after that which is lost, until he find it? And when he hath found it, he layeth it on his shoulders, rejoicing. And when he cometh home, he calleth together his friends and neighbors, saying unto them, Rejoice with me; for I have found my sheep which was lost. I say unto you, that likewise joy shall be in heaven over one sinner that repenteth, more than over ninety and nine just persons, which need no repentance."

One sinner that repenteth.

I still think about Scott from time to time, of course, and I continue to pray for him. I wonder if he ever thinks about Laci, or about Conner, or about all the people he hurt and left behind. Does he feel remorse? Does he care? Is he capable of caring?

I sometimes wonder if he thinks about me. I wonder if he resents me for having gone to the police, and for having done my part—and perhaps more than my part—to see that justice was served.

For as long as I live, I will never forget Gloria's words: "The day you went to the police, you became Laci's voice."

I wish there had never been any need for me to become Laci's voice. I wish I had never met Scott Peterson. I wish Scott and Laci had remained together, and been happy together, and raised their son together. Conner would have been almost two by now.

I wish I knew what happened inside Scott's tormented soul, so that I could at least try to be-gin to understand it. I often think back to that conversation we had on that cold, long ago January day:

"You say you can't tell me, you want to tell me in person. At what point are you going to tell me in person, Scott?"

"Once we find her . . . Once we find her, I will be able to explain everything to you."

I am no longer waiting for an explanation. I have moved on, and I have my whole life ahead of me.

In the Bible (Jeremiah 29:11) God says, "I know what I am planning for you . . . I have good plans for you, not plans to hurt you. I will give you hope and a good future."

I believe this. I believe it with all my heart. Whatever God has in store for me, I am ready.

On March 16, 2005, Scott Peterson was sentenced to death by lethal injection for the murders of his wife and unborn son.

ACKNOWLEDGMENTS

....

I have a great many people to thank.

To my family, Brenda and Mike, and Ron and Sonja, thank you for being there when I needed you most. I will be forever grateful. To my grandmother, Betty, who has been a best friend to me throughout my life, a big hug. To Jason, who proudly served in Iraq.

Thanks to Dave Markovich, a true friend and a great source of support during those difficult months, and a special thanks to his parents, Mary Jane and Frank, who are defined by their selflessness and generosity.

To Gloria Allred and Nathan Goldberg, my deepest gratitude for everything. When we first met, you were simply two brilliant attorneys. Today you are family. There will always be a place for you in my heart.

To the women of North Park Community Church: thank you for not judging me, and for your unconditional love. And thanks also for your prayers.

To all the other people who prayed for me,

ACKNOWLEDGMENTS

and who sent me cards and letters and e-mails of
support and encouragement, I'm sorry I couldn't
answer you individually. But I want to thank you
now: your kind words helped me through a very
difficult time.

To my colleagues at work: you protected me and
respected my privacy. I am immensely grateful.

To my friend Cynthia, who has been there for
me from the beginning, a million thank-yous.
You are a beautiful human being. I am here for
you always.

A big, heartfelt thanks to Detective Jon
Buehler, who took my statement that very first
morning and held my hand through the difficult
weeks and months ahead. You were like a big
brother to me. Thank you for listening, and
thank you for all your good advice. Thanks also
to the men and women of the Modesto Police
Department, for their support and kindness.

To Judith Regan, my publisher, and to Aliza
Fogelson, my editor, many thanks for believing
in me, and for letting me tell my story, my way.

To Pablo Fenjves, all my gratitude for your
hard work and total dedication to this project.

To Nina Skahan Sheffield—a big hug. Thank you
for your kind heart, your patience, and your guidance as we read and reread the manuscript.

Finally, a special thanks to my children, my
two little blessings, Ayiana and Justin. I love you
more than you can imagine.

CHAPTER

IV

....

*"Oh my God! Laci's baby is due
on my birthday!"*